VICTORY IN MOUNTAINS AND VALLEYS

MAKE EVERY DAY COUNT

BRUCE R. WITT

ISBN: 978-0-9965714-9-4

Unless otherwise noted, Scripture quotations are from the NEW AMERICAN STANDARD BIBLE®, Copyright © 1960, 1962, 1963, 1968, 1971, 1972, 1973, 1975, 1977, 1995 by The Lockman Foundation. Used by permission.

Scripture quotations marked (ESV) are from the The Holy Bible, English Standard Version. ESV® Text Edition: 2016. Copyright © 2001 by Crossway Bibles, a publishing ministry of Good News Publishers.

Scripture quotations marked (MSG) are from The Message. Copyright © 1993, 1994, 1995, 1996, 2000, 2001, 2002. Used by permission of NavPress Publishing Group.

Scripture quotations marked (NIV) are from THE HOLY BIBLE, NEW INTERNATIONAL VERSION®, NIV® Copyright © 1973, 1978, 1984, 2011 by Biblica, Inc.® Used by permission. All rights reserved worldwide.

Scripture quotations marked (NKJV) are from the New King James Version®. Copyright © 1982 by Thomas Nelson. Used by permission. All rights reserved.

Scripture quotations marked (NLT) are from Holy Bible, New Living Translation, copyright © 1996, 2004, 2015 by Tyndale House Foundation. Used by permission of Tyndale House Publishers, Inc., Carol Stream, Illinois 60188. All rights reserved.

Scripture quotations marked (RSV) are fromRevised Standard Version of the Bible, copyright © 1946, 1952, and 1971 the Division of Christian Education of the National Council of the Churches of Christ in the United States of America. Used by permission. All rights reserved.

Published by Leadership Revolution Inc. Learn more at www.LeadershipRevolution.us

Copy Editing and Interior Layout: James Armstrong, Upwrite Publishing

Cover Design: Michael Sean Allen

Leadership Revolution, Inc.
Bruce Witt, President
4465 Nassau Way
Marietta, GA 30068
678-637-9890
Bruce@LeadershipRevolution.us
www.LeadershipRevolution.us

November 2018 Printing

CONTENTS

VICTORY IN MOUNTAINS AND VALLEYS

Introduction

VICTORY IN MOUNTAINS AND VALLEYS

"Who shall separate us from the love of Christ? Shall tribulation, or distress, or persecution, or famine, or nakedness, or danger, or sword?...No, despite all these things, overwhelming victory is ours through Christ, who loved us" (Romans 8:35 ESV, 8:37 NLT).

Everyone faces mountains and valleys in life, that's a given. The question is, how do we experience victory in them? The short answer? We can have triumph in Christ in every circumstance! Is this too good to be true? Is it some overly positive mental attitude, or can it be a reality?

As we see in Romans 8:37 above, God's Word assures us that we can live victoriously in any situation, whether challenging or uplifting. The outside world need not define or dictate to us how we live nor should it frame our perspective about life.

This is a book about living with hope in life's difficulties, making progress all the while. It will offer a perspective about how to grow whether you're in the valley or on the mountaintop. Moreover, it will direct us to a path of increasing fruitfulness today and a rewarding eternity with Jesus Christ Himself. We will discover answers to questions such as: How do we handle pain and heartache in life? How do we finish well? What difference will we have made? What of lasting value will we have to show for our labor and effort?

This book is going to take you on an expedition where you will come to understand the mountains and valleys you personally face, where you

1

are today, how do you grow, and how you can move forward with an eye to a life well lived. Finally, these thoughts will challenge you to become more proactive and make life choices that bring joy to your journey and ensure you will make a permanent impact on the world around you. We all realize that that life in this world is short, and it seems to rush by at an ever-increasing speed. Therefore we must embrace the road ahead whole-heartedly and actively engage a purposeful life before it passes us by.

Bruce Witt

Chapter 1

OUR JOURNEY THROUGH LIFE

WE FACE TROUBLING TIMES

We face a world in chaos where the spiritual warfare between forces of light and world darkness is escalating every day. Paul reminded his protégé, Timothy, of this very fact: *"Realize this, that in the last days difficult times will come"* (2 Timothy 3:1). And he exhorts the Ephesian believers: *"Wake up from your sleep...make the most of every chance you get. These are desperate times!"* (MSG) And in another translation: *"Awake, sleeper, and arise from the dead, and Christ will shine on you. Therefore be careful how you walk, not as unwise men but as wise, making the most of your time, because the days are evil"* (Ephesians 5:14-16).

And Jesus tells us in John 16:33, *"These things I have spoken to you, so that in Me you may have peace. In the world you have tribulation, but take courage; I have overcome the world."*

These verses certainly describe the times in which we live. From financial uncertainty to political instability, from physical war to cyber war, troubles abound. Every person faces both personal and macro struggles whether relationally, spiritually, or physically. The answers and solutions we receive from the world (government, business world, media, and education, to name a few of the world's voices) usually result in more confusion and add to our difficulty, pain, and discouragement. After desperately searching for a life of peace and enjoyment, many people are losing hope in life and are seeking escape by some form of "medication"—money, possessions, pleasure, sex, drugs, power, etc.

HOPE FOR THE ROAD AHEAD

Yet hope provides a critical framework for life. The idea of hope looks at today and the future at the same time and gives us a reason to press forward. Hope, when founded on truth and reality, provides both motivation and a clearer perspective about the future.

Tim Keller, one of today's most influential pastors, has said, "We're having a crisis of hope in our world." We would all agree our world is becoming more polarized, strained, and vitriolic. Yet, how can we find what we need to keep looking toward a better future?

Consider these quotes from over the centuries:

"While there's life, there's hope." (Marcus Tullius Cicero, in 60 B.C.)

"Everything that is done in this world is done by hope." (Martin Luther, in the 1500s)

"Hope means hoping when things are hopeless, or it is no virtue at all....As long as matters are really hopeful, hope is mere flattery or platitude; it is only when everything is hopeless that hope begins to be a strength." (G. K. Chesterton, an English philosopher in the late 1900s)

"Christian hope isn't a feeling. And it's not wishful thinking. Hope comes from the certainty of God's promises." (Charles Colson, late 20th century)

REALITY

While the lack of hope appears to loom large today, in fact it has been eroding for decades, slipping away a small piece at a time almost unnoticed. As we look back, we can see how the primary elements of absolutes upon which hope is built began to break down.

4

1940s–1950s

In these decades we saw much of the world enmeshed in World War II, followed closely by the Korean War. With the extreme loss of life, total destruction of cities and countries, and the unfiltered power of evil, the sense of "where is God in all of this suffering" began to chip away at the God–fearing heritage that America had been built upon. Belief in an all-loving God began to be seriously questioned and the percentage of people going to church began a steady decline. In addition, these wars and their aftermath shook to the core our somewhat innocent confidence in "God and country" and authority in general.

1960s–1970s

The next two decades saw our culture marked by an all-out rebellion against any authority or societal structure, including the rejection of the government and the breakdown of the family as we once knew it. This rebellion was marked an explosion of drugs, sex, and violence. Our sense of meaning and purpose began to crumble because the "individual" became paramount with its idolizing of self. The "me" generation was launched. Our view of helping and serving others slipped away, and each individual became the center of his or her own world rather than living for a cause greater than self.

1980s–1990s

During these decades we saw the disintegration of morality and a further breakdown of relationships. Sex was substituted for true love and divorce grew and cohabitation became the norm. Sex outside of marriage was presumed to be fine as long as it was consensual, giving rise to a total lack of commitment. The idea of what was right and wrong became relative according to each person, erasing moral absolutes.

2000s–2010s

Over these last two decades we have experienced the abandonment of reason and civility. The environment of relativism that started in the previous time frame has grown exponentially. Since my "truth" is as good as yours, we live in a virtual lawless frame of mind, with even government ignoring the enforcement of laws, and protestors vilifying law enforcement officers. The polarization created in the political world has slipped into all walks of life, where vulgar tweets and putdowns are the norm. There is no longer dialogue and civil conversation.

This all can look quite depressing. Over the last two generations the elements that normally would give a person hope (a sense of a transcendent, all-loving God, innocence, authority, structure, a sense of meaning in life, morality, relationships, ability to reason and having a culture of civility) have seriously eroded, collapsed, or become nonexistent. Yet over this period many have sought to put their hope in money, government, education, pleasure, and possessions—none of which offers any lasting value.

On top of this loss of hope, we still face critical problems in our world that include: ongoing large- and small-scale conflicts/wars, poverty, government corruption, compromised food and water security, religious conflicts and fanaticism, a lack of education, and lack of economic and employment opportunities.

The only good that can come from all of these challenges and problems is we will realize sooner than later that the hope we seek is not found in ourselves, our money, our hard work, religion, or in the world system. The only real hope must be found in someone who transcends us and our world—Jesus Christ.

THE HOPE OF CHRIST

If our hope is founded on Christ, and if we are to live out this hope in order to make an impact in our world, we must also realize that the opportunities for our lives to make a difference are rapidly escaping. We must stop, face our mountains and valleys, and make every day count. Tim Keller not only has diagnosed the issue of our day, he also gives a solution, consider the following quotes from him:

"We need a living hope to get through life and endure suffering. A living hope enables us to have both sorrow and joy. Our living hope is an inheritance achieved for us by Christ."

"Because of Jesus—there is always hope, even in the darkest moments of your life."

"The whole world is going to be redeemed. Jesus is going to redeem spirit and body, reason and emotion, people and nature. There is no part of reality for which there is no hope."

"You and I are unavoidably and irreducibly hope-based creatures. We are controlled not how we live now, but what we think will happen later. Christian hope has to do with the ultimate future, not the immediate.

"Jesus is the true and better Jonah who was cast out into the storm so that we could be brought in."

"Biblical hope is life changing certainty about the future... being certain about the future in a way that affects how you live now."

If we are going to take on life's mountains and valleys, we will absolutely need an engaged hope that will fuel our faith so that we bear God-honoring fruit and finish well.

OBSERVATIONS ABOUT THE JOURNEY— THRIVING OR SURVIVING?

It is vitally important to know the "why" of our journey to live life to the fullest. Our perspective on the "why" of life gives us the motivation to persevere especially in difficulties. Our "why" provides a foundation that gives in multiple ways: Provides Hope, Clarifies Perspective and Focus, Guides the Journey, Restores Losses, Overcomes the Trials, Deepens Relationships, Multiplies Impact, and Transforms your Story.

We come back to Romans 8:37, *"No, despite all these things, over-whelming victory is ours through Christ, who loved us"* (NLT). That verse becomes an anchor and a beacon of hope as we travel along the way. Consider the wisdom in the following quotes that address the tension found in the journey in good and challenging times.

> *"We want Christ to hurry and calm the storm, He wants us to find Him in the midst of it first. No matter whose fault, God sends us through storms so we can land in a place we never would have otherwise."*
>
> — Beth Moore

> *"If we are following Christ, we are headed for home, but there are stages along the way and lessons to be learned. To follow Christ is to move into territory that is unknown to us and to count on His purposeful guidance, His grace when we go off the path, and His presence when we feel alone. It is to learn to respond to God's providential care in deepening ways and to accept the pilgrim character of earthly existence with its uncertainties, setbacks, disappointments, surprises, and joys. It is to remember we are in a process of conformity to the image of Christ so we can love and serve others along the way."*
>
> — Ken Boa

This journey is not for the casual observer or the faint of heart. We are all called to make a difference and take on the challenges that come our way. God has great things in store each of us who will grow, follow, and persevere. We make the choices that will help us to finish well or lead us into the proverbial ditch.

ENCOURAGEMENT ALONG THE WAY:

- Perspective offers hope, encouragement, and direction. Keep looking up and looking beyond.

- Knowing where you are in life allows you to grow and take steps of faith. You see how far you have come and what lies ahead.
- Finishing well is a lifelong process. Few finish well because they stop short, fall in the ditch, go alone, or won't pay the price.
- Embrace having an eternal purpose and impact. Motivate and prioritize your choices by investing in eternity, it lasts longer than the temporal. Treasure in heaven is better than treasure on earth.
- Reshape/transform your broken story by embedding it in God's grand story.
- See and experience Christ working and living through you daily because He offers you grace, peace, joy, and contentment.

JOURNEYING ON LIFE'S ROAD

Ken Boa, in *Conformed to His Image*, observes this process:

> "Seen in this light, the primary point of this earthly existence is preparation for our eternal citizenship in heaven. It is to learn to respond to God's providential care in deepening ways and to accept the pilgrim character of earthly existence with its uncertainties, setbacks, disappointments, surprises, and joys. It is to remember that we are in a process of gradual conformity to the image of Christ so that we can love and serve others along the way.
>
> "In this life we stumble in many ways (James 3:2) because we are still in process—our sanctification is not yet complete. Sanctification is both an event (we were sanctified when we gave ourselves to Christ; 1 Corinthians 6:11) and a process (we are being sanctified; Romans 12:2; Philippians 2-3; 1 John 2:28). Spiritual formation is the lifelong process of becoming in our character and actions the new creations we already are in Christ (2 Corinthians 5:17); it is the working out of what God has already worked in us (Philippians 2:12-13)."

This journey is not a set of dos and don'ts that we rigidly follow; rather, it is a response to God's invitation to be a part of His family, so we may be growing, learning, and enjoying life from Him. The blessing is that we experience Him both in the journey and forever in the destination. Life is not easy; it is demanding and at times arduous. This life and our spiritual walk is a process with many turns, twists, and choices.

We must embrace the journey through life's ups and downs by growing in our walk with the Lord, being conformed to His image, becoming mature, and giving our lives away. While our individual journeys are unique, we still share many similarities in the hurdles and difficulties we face. Having a picture or map of the journey gives us perspective as well as helps us navigate the ups and downs along the way. We also can anticipate what lies ahead so we are not caught unaware. Each journey has the same home destination: eternal life in heaven with the Lord and His saints.

IN THE MIDDLE OF THE STORM

"When we long for life without difficulties, remind us that oaks grow strong in contrary winds and diamonds are made under pressure."
— Peter Marshall

"We want Christ to hurry and calm the storm, He wants us to find Him in the midst of it first. No matter whose fault, God sends us through storms so we can land in a place we never would have otherwise."
— Beth Moore

"Pain insists upon being attended to. God whispers to us in our pleasures, speaks in our consciences, but shouts in our pains. It is his megaphone to rouse a deaf world."
— C. S. Lewis

Look around you. Depending on your vantage point you may see incredible cities and wealth, see the great good people are doing, and be amazed by science and technology. Or you may see devastating suffering, people in poverty starving and without hope. Good and evil, joy and pain exist side by side in any part of the world you call home. We often wish for a world without problems, yet it does not exist; there will always be storms to weather. We all are either in a storm, just coming out of one or getting ready to encounter one.

Consider the account of Jesus walking on the water in the midst of a storm. *"But the boat was already a long distance from the land, battered by the waves; for the wind was contrary. And in the fourth watch of the night He came to them, walking on the sea. When the disciples saw Him walking on the sea, they were terrified, and said, 'It is a ghost!' And they cried out in fear. But immediately Jesus spoke to them, saying, 'Take courage, it is I; do not be afraid.'*

"Peter said to Him, 'Lord, if it is You, command me to come to You on the water.' And He said, 'Come!' And Peter got out of the boat, and walked on the water and came toward Jesus. But seeing the wind, he became frightened, and beginning to sink, he cried out, 'Lord, save me!' Immediately Jesus stretched out His hand and took hold of him, and said to him, 'You of little faith, why did you doubt?' When they got into the boat, the wind stopped. And those who were in the boat worshiped Him, saying, 'You are certainly God's Son!'" (Matthew 14:24-33).

As the storm was raging, the disciples were emotional and fearful, then the Lord came, pursuing and inviting the disciples not to fear. The Lord is also doing the same for us in the storms we face. The question becomes, What is our first response: fear, anxiety, or faith? As we step out of the boat, do we keep our eyes on the Lord, or are we drawn to the outward circumstances? If we focus on the surroundings, we will sink and the Lord will have to reach out, catch, and guide us as He did for Peter.

Chapter 2

THE REALITY ROAD

WAKE UP TO THE REALITY OF THE DAY

Every day we face both external and internal forces through which we must navigate. The external forces are largely beyond our control. They include the world forces of darkness and the attacks of Satan, as well as global factors such as famine, physical wars, trade wars, and financial tensions. Crime, poverty, and family disintegration that plague our communities are also a part of these external forces. In addition, rapid growth in technology and globalization quickens life's pace and drives us toward greater complexity. These challenges are increasing and will continue to be daunting obstacles going forward. In short, the spiritual battle rages on, evil is taking off the mask and is affecting all of us. This is a sobering state of affairs! We must be awake and be aware of the issues of the day in order to prepare and take action. We must not be deceived, distracted, or in denial. These forces are real.

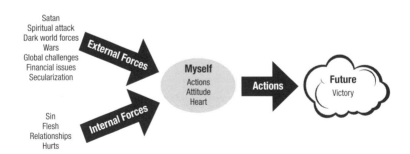

The internal forces are just as formidable. First, there is our daily battle with the "flesh." On top of this we have a list of influences that weigh us down and cause us to stumble:

- Personal tensions – Rising Debt, Greed, Job issues, Health, etc.
- Financial burden – debt/bondage, no spending or saving plan, spend on self, hope in riches.
- Emotional Reactions – Fear, Anxiety, Bondage, Hurt, Loneliness, Oppression or Confusion.
- Emptiness from working in our strength – trying to be God-like (the first sin).
- Relationships that need help, resolution and healing.

As we acknowledge our problems, the goal is not for us to overcome them in our strength. It is only by the Lord working in and through us that we can safely traverse these times of evil and turmoil.

UNDERSTANDING THE TIMES

In order to stand against these challenges we need to gain a new perspective by looking at our realities from God's viewpoint. This understanding helps us see the context, the crisis, and the path forward. We need to consider what is God doing and to cultivate spiritual eyes to see Him at work. We are reminded that God speaks to us about the times in which we live.

We previously referenced this passage in Ephesians that instructs us to be careful how we walk, watching for pitfalls as we discern and follow God's will. *"Therefore be careful how you walk, not as unwise men but as wise, making the most of your time, because the days are evil. So then do not be foolish, but understand what the will of the Lord is. And do not get drunk with wine, for that is dissipation, but be filled with the Spirit, speaking to one another in psalms and hymns and spiritual songs, singing and making melody with your heart to the Lord; always giving thanks for all things in the name of our Lord Jesus Christ to God, even the Father"* (Ephesians 5:15-20).

The Bible describes the sons of Issachar as *"men who understood the times, with knowledge of what Israel should do"* (1 Chronicles 12:32). From these verses we see that it is possible to discern the signs of the times, to be a student of what is going on. In other words, we are to have our eyes open to the reality of the days in which we live so that we can exercise wisdom, not being naïve or fearful. We can't escape the evil and the challenges, but we can be prepared to take action.

RESPONDING VS. REACTING

When we let our emotions (fear, anger, or hurt) drive us or we allow ourselves to be in denial about the times in which we live, we are reacting to our circumstances. Both paths are equally destructive.

Faced with difficulty we generally ask one of two questions: "Why?" or "What?" The "Why" question is not the right question. If we are constantly asking "Why?" it will only lead us to demand from God an answer as if we were on His level, or as though we were some kind of victim. It's a reactionary question. Instead, the right question to ask is "What?" It's a responsive question. What is God teaching me? What do I learn? What direction or next step do I take? In any and every circumstance we must seek and trust the Lord to guide as well as strengthen us to make spiritually mature responses.

TAKING ACTION

As we encounter the storms of life, we cannot sit by passively and lament, "God is in control and there is nothing one can do." We must recognize what is going on, take time with the Lord, and then take action. *"...The people who know their God display strength and take action"* (Daniel 11:32b). *"Therefore prepare your minds for action, keep sober in spirit, fix your hope completely on the grace to be brought to you at the revelation of Jesus Christ"* (1 Peter 1:13).

Here are five key actions we can take that will lay a firm foundation for our journey through life.

1. **Receiving God's Love**

   Before we ever pursue the Lord, we are invited into an intimate relationship with God through His Son, Jesus Christ. The

15

Lord unconditionally loves us more than we could ask or think. Receiving this kind of love begins to make us whole, healing the hurts of the past. We must receive His love before we can give it back or extend it to others.

2. **Loving the Lord**

    We love God by worship, praise and seeking to glorify Him in all that we think, do or say. We love the Lord by loving others and by sharing about Christ to others. We are called to love God with all of our heart, soul, mind and strength.

3. **Thanking the Lord**

    We are called to thank the Lord in everything. Note that in the following verses about thankfulness, there is no condition as to how good or bad the circumstances are—we are to thank the Lord continually. *"Be anxious for nothing, but in everything by prayer and supplication with thanksgiving let your requests be made known to God"* (Philippians 4:6). *"In everything give thanks; for this is God's will for you in Christ Jesus"* (1 Thessalonians 5:18). Thanking the Lord is one of the first steps we should take. We will receive a great blessing in doing so.

4. **Believing in God's Promises**

    Take some time to reflect on what God promises to each of us. These are especially encouraging when we are in a struggle or battle. These promises are a firm foundation for the working out of our faith. These are blessings we receive in our brokenness.

Reference	Blessing
Deuteronomy 32:10-11	God watches over us and shields us in the difficulties.
Psalm 9:9-10	God is a refuge and a stronghold in times of trouble.
Psalm 46:1-3	God is a safe place and will help us when we need it.

Psalm 147:3	God heals the brokenhearted and binds up the wounded.
Isaiah 41:10	God will uphold us as we wait upon Him.
Lamentations 3:19-26, 33	God's love and compassion are new and never fail.
Romans 6:5	We are united with Him in death, and we will be united in His life.
Romans 8:18	Affliction is momentary and light in comparison to the glory we will receive.
Romans 8:28	God works all things for good according to His riches in glory.
1 Corinthians 10:13	God will make a way through the valley, a way of escape in temptation.
2 Corinthians 1:3-7	God comforts us out of His character.
2 Corinthians 4:16-18	God renews us in our difficulties. We receive an eternal weight of glory.
Philippians 4:13	We can do all things through Christ who strengthens us.
Hebrews 4:15-16	Christ has been through suffering and He will give us mercy and grace.
1 Peter 5:7	Cast all your cares upon Him because He cares for you.

5. **Applying God's Word**

    We don't have the power to change our stories of brokenness and hurt. The only way to change our story is to embed it in God's story. He can and will transform us in order to make something new and wonderful from our broken lives.

Start with examining your heart. Be ready to modify how you use money; often this is God's means to grow us and reveal to us where our hearts truly lie. Move out of chaos to order through the process of correction, instruction, and obedience.

- Seek the Lord in the challenges; call and pray to Him.
- Be encouraged. You are not alone.
- Start thanking Him in every situation.
- Help others in greater need. It helps us remove our focus from ourselves or our challenging circumstances.
- Begin a personal spiritual growth plan to prepare for difficult days ahead.
- Find an accountability partner to ask you the tough questions.
- Start with a personality assessment.
- Find someone who is going through difficult time (maybe more than yourself) and minister to them personally and practically.

Chapter 3

TRIUMPH IN TURBULENT TIMES

THE VICTORIOUS LIFE DEFINED

The victorious life is a life of victory **OVER** sin, self (flesh), Satan, and death. It is a life of freedom from the power of sin as well as freedom from the *penalty* of sin; a life that is not only "reconciled to God through the death of His Son," but a life that is also "saved by His life" (Romans 5:10).

Definition: Victory - An act of defeating an enemy or opponent in a battle. A success in a struggle against difficulties or an obstacle ending in such triumph. A success or superior position achieved. Antonyms: defeat, failure, quit, despair, doubt, uncertainty.

It is having victory **IN** the struggles, difficulties, battles, pain, trials, and uncertainty.

What victory is *not*

- It is not a life in which it is impossible to sin, but a life in which victory over sin is possible. The first is unobtainable in this life, but the second is attainable.
- It is not an abnormal life or a life to be enjoyed by just a few, but it is His provision for every Christian.
- It is not a life where there is no temptation, but a life where temptation is overcome (see Hebrews 4:15).
- It is not a life of outward victory only, but a life of inward victory as well.

19

- It is not a fully-grown life where further growth in grace is unnecessary or impossible.
- It is not positive mental attitude, dream, or an emotion.
- It is not worldly success or having an abundance of wealth/possessions.

Is it God's will that we should live such a life of victory? Has He made provision for each and all of His children to be victorious all along the line? If so, we sin against Him by accepting and being satisfied with anything less than His will. Is it God's will that we, His children, should live defeated lives? Is it necessary for us to be beset and overcome by such things as temper, touchiness, untruthfulness, and pride?

What victory *is*

- Victory is found only in the Lord, not is our strength, effort, or desires.
- Victory is realized by looking up, not by looking back, forward, or around.
- Victory is available in our daily battles and difficulties.
- Victory is available to every believer and realized by maturity and trust/hope.
- Victory is a resolve, courage, commitment, blessings, and an overcoming.
- Victory is a reality filled with hope and is expectant about the future.
- Victory is an eternal perspective and sees time/treasure from God's perspective.
- Victory is empowered by prayer.

SEIZING THE VICTORY

Victory is given by the Lord but must be seized or taken hold of. We must possess it. Here are five principles that will help you capture and live in victory.

1. **Christ leads us in victory and triumph.** Christ's leadership in our lives is based on knowing who we are in Christ, allowing Him to live in and through us.

    "But thanks be to God, who always leads us in triumph in Christ, and manifests through us the sweet aroma of the knowledge of Him in every place" (2 Corinthians 2:14).

2. **Jesus Christ is our source of victory.** Jesus has defeated Satan and death so they no longer have control or authority in our lives. Christ in us (Galatians 2:20) is the victory over sin and gives us the power over committing sins. We appropriate this victory through an intimacy and maturity with Christ.

    "Yours, O Lord, is the greatness and the power and the glory and the victory and the majesty, indeed everything that is in the heavens and the earth; Yours is the dominion, O Lord, and You exalt Yourself as head over all. Both riches and honor come from You, and You rule over all, and in Your hand is power and might; and it lies in Your hand to make great and to strengthen everyone" (1 Chronicles 29:11-12).

    "The horse is prepared for the day of battle, but victory belongs to the Lord" (Proverbs 21:31).

    "But in all these things we overwhelmingly conquer through Him who loved us" (Romans 8:37).

3. **Victory is given—it is a gift!** Victory is a gift to be received and not achieved. It is not on the basis of human effort. The only part we play is dying to self and stepping out in faith to receive this gift.

    "Thanks be to God, who gives us the victory through our Lord Jesus Christ. Therefore, my beloved brethren, be steadfast, immovable, always abounding in the work of the Lord, knowing that your toil is not in vain in the Lord" (1 Corinthians 15:57-58).

4. **We participate in the victory.** We are invited to be a part of the victory which reveals to us the part we play in the world and in relationship to other believers.

21

"For whatever is born of God overcomes the world; and this is the victory that has overcome the world—our faith" (1 John 5:4).

"Where there is no guidance the people fall, but in abundance of counselors there is victory" (Proverbs 11:14).

"For by wise guidance you will wage war, and in abundance of counselors there is victory" (Proverbs 24:6).

"Do you not know that those who run in a race all run, but only one receives the prize? Run in such a way that you may win" (1 Corinthians 9:24).

"Also if anyone competes as an athlete, he does not win the prize unless he competes according to the rules" (2 Timothy 2:5).

5. **Victory comes only through surrender.** Only as we give up (lose/surrender) our will can we enter into or gain what Christ has already made available. Jesus said:

"Whoever finds his life will lose it, and whoever loses his life for my sake will find it" (Matthew 10:39 ESV).

THE STORY OF PAUL

Consider the story of Paul recorded in Philippians 1:12-17, 21-23.

"Now I want you to know, brethren, that my circumstances have turned out for the greater progress of the gospel, so that my imprisonment in the cause of Christ has become well known throughout the whole praetorian guard and to everyone else, and that most of the brethren, trusting in the Lord because of my imprisonment, have far more courage to speak the word of God without fear. Some, to be sure, are preaching Christ even from envy and strife, but some also from good will; the latter do it out of love, knowing that I am appointed for the defense of the gospel; the former proclaim Christ out of selfish ambition rather than from pure motives, thinking to cause me distress in my imprisonment....

"For to me, to live is Christ and to die is gain. But if I am to

*live on in the flesh, this will mean fruitful labor for me; and I do
not know which to choose. But I am hard-pressed from both
directions, having the desire to depart and be with Christ, for
that is very much better."*

- The Lord allowed difficulties and difficult times into Paul's life. Paul saw a bigger picture—that either way, good or bad, circumstances can be used by the Lord.
- Jesus' life is the source of life, power, wisdom, vision, grace, and hope.
- Life challenges are not about you, they are about connecting with people.
- People are eternal—get your eyes off of yourself.
- People are your hope, joy, and crown of exultation.
- Difficulties invite community. Pursue others.

IMPLICATIONS – SO WHAT?

- While the victory is available to all, it is not realized by all. Thus, if we have or are experiencing the victory, we must be careful not to compare or compete with other believers thinking that we are further along or more mature. Conversely if we have struggles, we must not beat ourselves up as if we were nobodies. We all are children of the King. Don't compare with others.
- The struggles and battles are generally with the world, the flesh, and the devil. We do not have enough strength or wisdom to overcome the enemy. We must let the Lord fight our battles.
- The existence of pain, suffering, or trials is neither evidence of maturity or failure. We are fully loved and accepted by Christ, not on the basis of what we have done, but on the basis of what He has done.
- This victory of "appropriating the eternal life now" brings with it an additional eternal reward in heaven. This motivates or compels us to sacrifice today to gain in the future. "He is no fool who gives

up what he can not keep to gain what he can not lose" (Jim Elliot). How we live our life will impact others for eternity.

- For us to receive the gift of the victory we must be **FAT**—Faithful, Available, and Teachable. We must also be hungering and thirsting to grow in our walk with the Lord.

- The world tells us to win at all costs and that winners are better than losers. Jesus tells us to give up and lose our life in order to gain or have victory. By embracing this truth you will be going against the world and that can be a lonely road.

A life of victory and overcoming obstacles is available for every believer. Most people do not experience this reality due to unbelief, a lack of understanding, or fleshly entanglements. To be victorious in the outcome, we will look at four broad components that frame our life.

1. The first is "Clarifying Your Hope."

2. The second is "Finding Fulfillment" which includes the larger perspective of our ultimate meaning and purpose in life that provide a compass to guide us. These two principles lay the foundation for the heart of this book.

3. The third is "Living in Victory" which details the specific path that leads us through the eight mountains and valleys and what is takes to navigate form one to the next.

4. The final component is "Making a Difference" which challenges us to leave a legacy and live with eternity clearly in view.

The following devotional from Oswald Chambers describes this process in a very compelling way.

VISIONS BECOMING REALITY
The parched ground shall become a pool... ISAIAH 35:7
We always have a vision of something before it actually becomes real to us. When we realize that the vision is real, but is not yet real in us, Satan comes to us with his temptations, and we are inclined to say that there is no point in even trying

to continue. Instead of the vision becoming real to us, we have entered into a valley of humiliation.

Life is not as idle ore,
But iron dug from central gloom,
And battered by the shocks of doom
To shape and use.

God gives us a vision, and then He takes us down to the valley to batter us into the shape of that vision. It is in the valley that so many of us give up and faint. Every God-given vision will become real if we will only have patience. Just think of the enormous amount of free time God has! He is never in a hurry. Yet we are always in such a frantic hurry. While still in the light of the glory of the vision, we go right out to do things, but the vision is not yet real in us. God has to take us into the valley and put us through fires and floods to batter us into shape, until we get to the point where He can trust us with the reality of the vision. Ever since God gave us the vision, He has been at work. He is getting us into the shape of the goal He has for us, and yet over and over again we try to escape from the Sculptor's hand in an effort to batter ourselves into the shape of our own goal.

The vision that God gives is not some unattainable castle in the sky, but a vision of what God wants you to be down here. Allow the Potter to put you on His wheel and whirl you around as He desires. Then as surely as God is God, and you are you, you will turn out as an exact likeness of the vision. But don't lose heart in the process. If you have ever had a vision from God, you may try as you will to be satisfied on a lower level, but God will never allow it.

— My Utmost for His Highest, Updated Edition

Chapter 4

EXPERIENCING HOPE

"To live without Hope is to cease to live."
— Fyodor Dostoevsky

"You define life backwards and then live it forward."
— Søren Kierkegaard

"Our hope is in the power of God working through the hearts of people. And that's where our hope is in this country. And that's where our hope is in this life. As Christians, we have no reason to lack hope. Christ has shown the trustworthiness of God and of His Word. It's this Christian hope that gives us the joy, the self-sacrificial love, the boldness, and the endurance to carry on—even in tough times."
— Charles Colson

Our hope in Christ is that not only can we survive, but we can flourish. We can thrive, grow, multiply, and bear fruit in any circumstance because of His life in and through us, no matter any external gloom and doom. There is a great promise in John 16:33, *"These things I have spoken to you, so that in Me you may have peace. In the world you have tribulation, but take courage; I have overcome the world."* Christ is present to work in us and through us to give us an abundant life and experience victory.

Finding and living with hope is probably the greatest spiritual activity and discipline we can exercise. Hope motivates us; it focuses our attention

27

on the Lord and His character rather than on our circumstances. Hope offers perspective to make wise choices in order to journey on with a positive attitude versus being angry and bitter. Hope grows our faith and love so that others grow.

A biblical "hope" is that of certainty because it's based on God's immutable character. There is an assurance as to the result—it is a fact. Hope is the reason for our faith, for our life. We will see that this hope is reflected tangibly in how we handle our finances and motivates us to a lifestyle of contentment, generosity, and investing in eternity. *"Instruct those who are rich in this present world not to be conceited or to fix their hope on the uncertainty of riches, but on God, who richly supplies us with all things to enjoy. Instruct them to do good, to be rich in good works, to be generous and ready to share, storing up for themselves the treasure of a good foundation for the future, so that they may take hold of that which is life indeed"* (1 Timothy 6:17).

The quality of your life now and your life in eternity is primarily determined by your hope. Hope involves answering "why" we are here. It helps us determine what are our motivations; it guides us in setting direction and living out our priorities. What gives you passion and excitement? What inspires you? Ephesians 1:18-19 describes the hope of our calling, what we are giving our life to. *"I pray that the eyes of your heart may be enlightened, so that you will know what is the hope of His calling, what are the riches of the glory of His inheritance in the saints, and what is the surpassing greatness of His power toward us who believe. These are in accordance with the working of the strength of His might."*

> *"If faith is at war with fear, if catastrophe can turn from death to resurrection, if hope can triumph over despair ... if there was ever a time for the church to be the church, it is now."*
> — Charles Colson, Being the Body

WHAT IS HOPE?

The world considers hope wishful thinking, a feeling that what is wanted can be had or that events will turn out for the best. They define hope from a temporary or worldly view—"I hope this situation turns out like I want."

True hope is a confident assurance. Hope is the reason for our faith, for our life. Paul in his letter to the Colossians said that the Spirit of Jesus Christ in each believer is our hope. *"To them God has chosen to make known among the Gentiles the glorious riches of this mystery, which is Christ in you, the hope of glory"* (Colossians 1:27 NIV). We have the hope of life and eternity in us!

START WITH A FRESH PERSPECTIVE – SEEING FROM GOD'S VIEWPOINT

How we see things will either help us move forward or keep us stuck. Do we see our difficulties as challenges or opportunities? Our hope will influence our viewpoint. God encourages us to look up, *"Lift up your eyes to the sky, then look to the earth beneath; for the sky will vanish like smoke, and the earth will wear out like a garment and its inhabitants will die in like manner; but My salvation will be forever, and My righteousness will not wane"* (Isaiah 51:6).

Seeing from God's perspective raises our attention above the circumstances, allowing us to view both the horizon and the Lord at work. We see our hope being realized and thus our actions in the moment can be one of confidence and peace.

THE SOURCE OF HOPE – GOD'S CHARACTER, HIS PLAN, AND HIS SON

God's character is the ultimate source of our hope! He is unchanging, always loving, all-knowing, and all-powerful. This becomes the rock upon which we can build our lives, which is same rock Jesus described in the Sermon on the Mount (see Matthew 7:24-27).

In addition to character, God has a plan for this world and a purpose for our lives. This plan and purpose is articulated in the promise God has for His people: *"For I know the plans that I have for you,' declares the Lord, 'plans for welfare and not for calamity to give you a future and a hope. Then you will call upon Me and come and pray to Me, and I will listen to you. You will seek Me and find Me when you search for Me with all your heart. I will be found by you,' declares the Lord, 'and I will restore your fortunes and will gather you from all the nations and from all the places where I have driven you"* (Jeremiah 29:11-14).

Hope is not found in this world or the things of this world, its origin is solely in God the Father and the Lord Jesus Christ. We need to truly know God the Father and Jesus at a heart level in order to appropriate this hope.

HOPE IS THE MOTIVATION FOR MY FAITH

Much of our Christian teaching about living life centers on our faith, and rightfully so. We have our faith in Christ who provided us salvation. Faith defines our actions and how we live.

Where does faith comes from? Faith is a product of hope—*"Faith is the assurance of things hoped for, the conviction of things not seen"* (Hebrews 11:1). If you want to grow your faith, grow your hope. This comes as we gain a larger view of God, His character and the love with which He showers us. Hope grows as we recognize the infinite amount of grace that has been given to us and further consider that we deserved none of it.

Hope spurs us to action and to exercise faith. People move in the direction where they believe they will find gain. We invest where we think there will be a return. We all want to invest in what will last. The Scriptures are clear that there are only two things that will last—people and the Word of God. These are what we need to spend our time, talent, and treasure on. *"For who is our hope or joy or crown of exultation? Is it not even you, in the presence of our Lord Jesus at His coming?"* (1 Thessalonians 2:19). Are people your priority? How about God's Word?

HOPE IN DIFFICULTY

Hope and difficulty go hand in hand. Let us consider three aspects of how hope is helpful in our challenges.

Hope is an Anchor of the Soul. Hope is the anchor for us in the storm. It holds us secure and solid. *"In the same way God, desiring even more to show to the heirs of the promise the unchangeableness of His purpose, interposed with an oath, so that by two unchangeable things in which it is impossible for God to lie, we who have taken refuge would have strong encouragement to take hold of the hope set before us. This hope we have as an anchor of the soul, a hope both sure and steadfast and one which enters within the veil, where Jesus has entered as a forerunner for us..."* (Hebrews 6:17-20).

Hope is Clarified in the Difficulties. Hope is clarified in times of difficulty in order to sustain me in the good times. When the problems surround us we realize that not all things are important, truly only a few things are most critical. If one has a dying friend or is battling cancer, if my favorite sports team wins or loses becomes not so important. Thus we realize that the difficulties help order our priorities and life from a place of Christ-centeredness. *"We also exult in our tribulations, knowing that tribulation brings about perseverance; and perseverance proven character; and proven character, hope; and hope does not disappoint"* (Romans 5:3-5).

Afflictions Help Develop our Ministry. We see that God meets us and comforts us in our afflictions so we will be empathic and have an increased heart to minister to others in need. *"Blessed be the God and Father of our Lord Jesus Christ, the Father of mercies and God of all comfort, who comforts us in all our affliction so that we will be able to comfort those who are in any affliction with the comfort with which we ourselves are comforted by God. For just as the sufferings of Christ are ours in abundance, so also our comfort is abundant through Christ"* (2 Corinthians 1:3-5). People relate to us more in our pain than they do in our victories. We become real to them; Christians have the same struggles as the lost world—they just have a different hope. Pain is a gift of God so we can offer hope to others.

THE HOPE OF CHRIST IN YOU –
EXPERIENCING THE ABUNDANT LIFE

On many occasions the Bible describes that Christ is our life. If Christ is our life, this is much more than being Christ-like. To be Christ-like is to look like Christ in our actions, and attitudes. To have Christ as our life is to realize He lives in us in the form of the Spirit and we take on His strength, His power, and His wisdom. Take note of the following verses and consider what they say about the source and substance of our life. This is what Paul was saying that for him to live is Christ (Christ working in and through him). This is radically different from trying hard to imitate Christ or to do what Christ did in our own strength.

> *"For to me, to live is Christ, and to die is gain"* (Philippians 1:21).
>
> *"I have been crucified with Christ; and it is no longer I who live, but Christ lives in me; and the life which I now live in the flesh I live by faith in the Son of God, who loved me and gave Himself up for me"* (Galatians 2:20).
>
> *"The thief comes only to steal and kill and destroy; I came that they may have life, and have it abundantly"* (John 10:10).
>
> *"For you have died and your life is hidden with Christ in God. When Christ, who is our life, is revealed, then you also will be revealed with Him in glory"* (Colossians 3:3-4).
>
> *"Jesus said to him, 'I am the way, and the truth, and the life; no one comes to the Father but through Me'"* (John 14:6).
>
> *"This is eternal life, that they know [Me]..."* (John 17:3).

We must move from focusing on being Christ-like to possessing Christ as life. He is the Christian life; it is not by works. It is lived by yielding to Him and stepping out in faith. For Christ to be alive in us and be real in our everyday life, we must know Him at a heart level, take hold of who we are in Him, and allow Him to be released through us in our actions. This process is called "appropriating" Christ.

"In Christ" we have a new identity, and because of this Christ changes us. He has allowed your difficulties and your difficult times; He will see you through them. We can do all things through Christ who strengthens us (see Philippians 4:13).

> *Your real, new self (which is Christ's and also yours, and yours just because it is His) will not come as long as you are looking for it. It will come when you are looking for Him....Give up yourself. And you will find your real self. Lose your life and you will save it....Keep back nothing. Nothing that you have not given away will ever be really yours. Nothing in you that has not died will ever be raised from the dead. Look for yourself and you will find in the long run only hatred, loneliness, despair, rage, ruin, and decay. But look for Christ and you will find Him, and with Him everything else will be thrown in."*
>
> *– C. S. Lewis, Mere Christianity*

The quality of your life now and your life in eternity is primarily determined by hope.

Hope helps determine the quality of life today and in eternity by giving us a reason to live, by motivating us to invest and give wisely, to exercise faith in a right direction and to hold us fast in the storms of life. This is especially true when it comes to our stewarding the resources God has given us. Hope motivates us to grow spiritually and press through difficult times.

A. W. Tozer put it well in his devotional classic, *The Knowledge of the Holy*:

> *"The days of the years of our lives are few, and swifter than a weaver's shuttle. Life is a short and fevered rehearsal for a concert we cannot stay to give. Just when we appear to have*

attained some proficiency we are forced to lay our instruments down. There is simply not time enough to think, to become, to perform what the constitution of our natures indicates we are capable of....How completely satisfying to turn from our limitations to a God who has none? Eternal years lie in His heart. For Him time does not pass, it remains; and those who are in Christ share with Him all the riches of limitless time and endless years."

Hope is a motivator

Our hope is what motivates your life and your walk. In the following verses we how hope gives energy and expression to our faith.

"Therefore, since we have such a hope, we are very bold" (2 Corinthians 3:12 NIV).

"We through the Spirit, by faith, are waiting for the hope of righteousness" (Galatians 5:5).

"Remembering before our God and Father your work of faith and labor of love and steadfastness of hope in our Lord Jesus Christ" (1 Thessalonians 1:3 ESV).

"God did this so that, by two unchangeable things in which it is impossible for God to lie, we who have fled to take hold of the hope offered to us may be greatly encouraged" (Hebrews 6:18 NIV).

"Be joyful in hope, patient in affliction, faithful in prayer" (Romans 12:12 NIV).

"I pray that the eyes of your heart may be enlightened, so that you will know what is the hope of His calling, what are the riches of the glory of His inheritance in the saints, and what is the surpassing greatness of His power toward us who believe" (Ephesians 1:18-19).

Hope does not disappoint

"And hope does not disappoint, because the love of God has been poured out within our hearts through the Holy Spirit who was given to us" (Romans 5:5).

Hope is what the world is looking for

Let your hope be so attractive that you will be compelled to share Christ with others. *"But in your hearts honor Christ the Lord as holy, always being prepared to make a defense to anyone who asks you for a reason for the hope that is in you; yet do it with gentleness and respect"* (1 Peter 3:15 ESV).

Hope helps make a difference in your life

- Hope is the difference between stepping out and never starting.
- Hope is the difference between persevering and quitting.
- Hope is the difference between sacrificing and holding on.
- Hope is the difference between arriving and wandering aimlessly.
- Hope is the difference between living and dying.
- Hope is living at a level beyond survival—Peace, Freedom, Sacrifice.

Chapter 5

FINDING FULFILLMENT IN GOD'S PURPOSE

We have seen that we can have victory and hope in Christ regardless of our circumstances. Building on this, we are invited to be a part of God's purposes and plans. He has a purpose and future for us. Note Ephesians 2:10, *"For we are His workmanship, created in Christ Jesus for good works, which God prepared beforehand so that we would walk in them. For we are His workmanship, created in Christ Jesus for good works, which God prepared beforehand so that we would walk in them."*

When we discover God's purposes and then our unique purpose, we gain a sense of fulfillment and life has new meaning. We begin to understand how the ups and owns of life are all a part of God's bigger plan. We then can embrace the promise, *"And we know that God causes all things to work together for good to those who love God, to those who are called according to His purpose.... What then shall we say to these things? If God is for us, who is against us?"* (Romans 8:28, 31).

KNOWING GOD AND HIS PURPOSES

This fulfillment that comes from knowing we are a part of God's larger plan begins with knowing Him and learning that He is all-loving and full of grace. The Lord knows where we are and what we are going through. He does not leave us alone, nor does He withhold his unfailing love and grace in our troubles. The Lord is not asleep at the switch—He is in charge. Yet, the Lord will use trials to mold, shape, and restore us to so that we can know Him and walk with Him. He uses pain to correct us, prune us, and mature us. He truly has our best interests at heart. *"Consider it all joy, my brethren, when you encounter various trials, knowing that the testing of your faith produces endurance. And let endurance have its perfect result, so that you may be perfect and complete, lacking in nothing"* (James 1:2-4).

God allows difficulties in order for us to stand out and give hope to others. We are to be a light in the darkness so that we can relate to the world and the world can relate to us. *"Let your light shine before men in such a way that they may see your good works, and glorify your Father who is in heaven"* (Matthew 5:16). Through this process we are able to minister the gospel and Christ to those in need. *"Blessed be the God and Father of our Lord Jesus Christ, the Father of mercies and God of all comfort, who comforts us in all our affliction so that we will be able to comfort those who are in any affliction with the comfort with which we ourselves are comforted by God"* (2 Corinthians 1:3-4). This verse is very clear: The Lord will meet us and comfort us in our need so that we are able to comfort others in any need. Our pain is a connection to a lost and dying world, it allows us to be real and authentic in our struggles. This is actually attractive to people in need and will cause the lost to ask what makes us different. Consider this devotional from Oswald Chambers that reinforces this perspective.

GOD'S PURPOSE OR MINE?

He made His disciples get into the boat and go before Him to the other side... MARK 6:45

We tend to think that if Jesus Christ compels us to do something and we are obedient to Him, He will lead us to great success. We should never have the thought that our dreams of success are God's purpose for us. In fact, His purpose may be exactly the opposite. We have the idea that God is leading us toward a particular end or a desired goal, but He is not. The question of whether or not we arrive at a particular goal is of little importance, and reaching it becomes merely an episode along the way. What we see as only the process of reaching a particular end, God sees as the goal itself.

What is my vision of God's purpose for me? Whatever it may be, His purpose is for me to depend on Him and on His power now. If I can stay calm, faithful, and unconfused while in the middle of the turmoil of life, the goal of the purpose of God is being accomplished in me. God is not working toward a particular finish— His purpose is the process itself. What He desires for me is that I see "Him walking on the sea" with no shore, no success, nor goal in sight, but simply having the absolute certainty that everything is all right because I see "Him walking on the sea" (Mark 6:49). It is the process, not the outcome, that is glorifying to God.

God's training is for now, not later. His purpose is for this very minute, not for sometime in the future. We have nothing to do with what will follow our obedience, and we are wrong to concern ourselves with it. What people call preparation, God sees as the goal itself.

God's purpose is to enable me to see that He can walk on the storms of my life right now. If we have a further goal in mind, we are not paying enough attention to the present time. However, if we realize that moment-by-moment obedience is the goal, then each moment as it comes is precious.

– My Utmost for His Highest, Updated Edition

LIVING IN VICTORY

If we are to live in victory we must understand and see life as a series of mountains and valleys that are connected and carry us to a deeper relationship with God. We then can make sense of the pain, which at times seems random, and realize that although we enjoy the mountaintops we can't live there.

Our progress on this trail takes time and has both hidden dangers and blessings. All start the journey, yet few finish well. At the heart of the journey are eight lessons of navigating the ups and downs we will face. These lessons give us an unusual insight into assessing ourselves and committing to a growth process that will help us flourish.

EIGHT LESSONS TO VICTORY

	Lesson	Mountain or Valley
1	In Chaos, wake up and own it.	Mountain of Wilderness
2	Surrender is the first step to victory.	Valley of Death
3	Order requires giving up ownership and doing the right things.	Mountain of Common Sense
4	Establish the depth of your walk through pruning and abiding.	Valley of Dependence
5	Maturity seeks God's will only, exercising His wisdom fully.	Mountain of Wisdom
6	Sacrifice puts others ahead of self through serving.	Valley of Others
7	Eternity is a reality of life that is received today and lived forever.	Mountain of the Kingdom
8	Take action and persevere, motivated by hope to finish well.	Valley of Faithfulness

An underlying theme on the journey is that we can be transformed by the living God to follow wherever He leads. We are called to be an active participant in the process, not just a fan in the bleachers. This transformation shapes both our new identity and the subsequent actions. We come to understand that the Lord is more interested in a relationship and who we are than in what we do.

Finally, examine the legacy we will leave—is it fruitful or not? We are confronted with the idea that the process has real and eternal consequences. Knowing we are called to a hope motivates us to walk by faith, to press on and persevere.

HEARING GOD'S MESSAGE

We began with a quote from C. S. Lewis: "God shouts in our pains. It is his megaphone to rouse a deaf world." The Lord uses our pain for a purpose, and as we have said, he uses it to mold and correct us. He also uses it to speak to our hearts when we are in need. Jesus understood this well: *"Jesus stood and cried out, saying, 'If anyone is thirsty, let him come to Me and drink. He who believes in Me, as the Scripture said, "From his innermost being will flow rivers of living water"'"* (John 7:37-38). We see the Lord reaching out to the thirsty—those who need the Lord and His presence. God is calling and inviting. Are we listening? Are we taking note? As you encounter problems, begin to take note of what is the message God is trying to speak to your heart.

Hearing leads to biblical action. God calls to us and wants to prepare us for troubling times ahead. Matthew 7:24-27, *"Therefore everyone who hears these words of Mine and acts on them, may be compared to a wise man who built his house on the rock. And the rain fell, and the floods came, and the winds blew and slammed against that house; and yet it did not fall, for it had been founded on the rock. Everyone who hears these words of Mine and does not act on them, will be like a foolish man who built his house on the sand. The rain fell, and the floods came, and the winds blew and slammed against that house; and it fell—and great was its fall."* Which rock are you building on?

EMBRACING THE PAIN

Paul reminds these believers that the conflict and pain they saw in him, they too must accept and endure. This would not be an option but a certainty. We all need to be reminded of this. Pain will come if we follow Christ, yet be encouraged because it has many redeeming qualities. Philippians 1:29-30, *"For to you it has been granted for Christ's sake, not only to believe in Him, but also to suffer for His sake, experiencing the same conflict which you saw in me, and now hear to be in me."* C. S. Lewis in his book, *The Problem of Pain*, says, "When pain is to be born, a little courage helps more than much knowledge, a little human sympathy more than much courage, and the least tincture of the love of God more than all."

As we approach the problem of pain, we make several observations:

1. Pain, difficulties, and struggles have existed since Adam & Eve and will not cease until Christ returns.
2. Pain has its origin in evil and/or sin. We live in a world where all is not well.
3. Every person experiences pain—it is universal. We all may not have happiness, we all will have pain.
4. Pain can be a warning signal of our limits; it highlights when we are approaching a problem.
5. Pain can be redemptive if seen from God's view. There are a number of blessings with pain.

Jesus was honest about pain. He told us the truth. He said we *will* have suffering in this world (see John 16:33). He didn't say you might—He said it is going to happen.

Dr. Ramesh Richard shares the following thoughts about pain:

1. Pain Connects…
   » Me to my human limitations as frail, mortal and impermanent
   » Me to my fellow suffers with understanding and compassion
   » Me to God in expectant prayer for healing and intervention
   » Me to certain Scriptures and biographies in a more alert manner.

2. Pain Cleanses
   » Me from dependence on idols
   » Me from all kinds of pride
   » Me from known sin through confession

3. Pain Corrects
   » My attitudes – like ingratitude, fear, resignation
   » My values – have I unintentionally accepted worldly values?
   » My behavior – pinpoints my rationalizations
   » My anxieties – will I trust the God who loves me?
4. Pain Clarifies
   » My beliefs – on what truths am I concentrating?
   » My activities – am I engaged in the right mix?
   » My priorities – what if pain should linger?
   » My adjustments – how do I adjust to loss?
5. Pain Confirms
   » God's providence in timing and intensity
   » The Father's goodness
   » Christ's presence
   » The Holy Spirit's power of resolve and triumph
   » God's inner supply of grace, joy, peace, and joy.

Part of the challenge with pain is that we don't see with God's eyes. *"Now we see things imperfectly, like puzzling reflections in a mirror, but then we will see everything with perfect clarity. All that I know now is partial and incomplete, but then I will know everything completely, just as God now knows me completely"* (1 Corinthians 13:12 NLT).

Lee Strobel offers us a reflection on pain and suffering that he calls "Five Points of Light."

Point of Light #1: God is not the creator of evil and suffering. God did not create evil and suffering. Now, it's true that he did create the potential for evil to enter the world, because that was the only way to create the potential for genuine goodness and love. But it was human beings, in our free will, who brought that potential evil into reality.

Point of Light #2: Though suffering isn't good, God can use it to accomplish good.

He does this by fulfilling His promise in Romans 8:28: "And we know that in all things God works for the good of those who love him, who have been called according to his purpose." Notice that the verse doesn't say God causes evil and suffering, just that he promises to cause good to emerge. God can use our suffering to draw us to Himself, to mold and sharpen our character, to influence others for Him—He can draw something good from our pain in a myriad of ways…if we trust and follow Him.

Point of Light #3: The day is coming when suffering will cease and God will judge evil.

God is actually delaying the consummation of history in anticipation that some of you will still put your trust in Him and spend eternity in heaven. He's delaying everything out of His love for you. 2 Peter 3:9 says: "The Lord is not slow in keeping His promise, as some understand slowness. He is patient with you, not wanting anyone to perish, but everyone to come to repentance." To me, that's evidence of a loving God, that He would care that much for you.

Point of Light #4: Our suffering will pale in comparison to what God has in store for his followers.

God promises a time when there will be no more crying, no more tears, no more pain and suffering, when we will be reunited with God in perfect harmony, forever. Let the words of First Corinthians 2:9 soak into your soul: "No eye has seen, no ear has heard, no mind has conceived what God has prepared for those who love him." That's absolutely breathtaking, isn't it?

Point of Light #5: We decide whether to turn bitter or turn to God for peace and courage.

God offers us the two very things we need when we're hurting: peace to deal with our present and courage to deal with our future. How? Because he has conquered the world! Through His own suffering and death, He has deprived this world of its ultimate power over you. Suffering doesn't have the last word anymore. Death doesn't have the last word anymore. God has the last word!

Our application could be to reflect how God has used your suffering to shape and grow you. Share this with another. Don't go alone. Focusing on your pain will isolate you and can take you out of the journey. Don't live in denial. From the depths of a Nazi death camp, Corrie ten Boom wrote these words: "No matter how deep our darkness, He is deeper still. Every tear we shed becomes his tear."

Chapter 6

CLIMBING MOUNTAINS & LIVING IN VALLEYS

"God allows us to experience the low points of life in order to teach us lessons that we could learn in no other way...We can ignore even pleasure. But pain insists upon being attended to. God whispers to us in our pleasures, speaks in our conscience, but shouts in our pains: it is his megaphone to rouse a deaf world."

– C. S. Lewis

"Climb mountains not so the world can see you, but so you can see the world."

– David McCullough, Jr.

Ken Boa discusses the road we will travel together:

"We are travelers on a quest, a voyage, an odyssey, a pilgrimage. If we are following Christ, we are headed for home, but there are stages along the way and lessons to be learned. This is why it is a mistake to view the spiritual life as a static condition or a state of being that can be attained by a combination of technique and information. To follow Christ is to move into territory that is unknown to us and to count on His purposeful guidance, His grace when we go off the path, and His presence when we feel alone. It is to learn to respond to God's providential care in deepening ways and to accept the pilgrim

character of earthly existence with its uncertainties, setbacks, disappointments, surprises, and joys. It is to remember that we are in a process of gradual conformity to the image of Christ so that we can love and serve others along the way."

We have set the stage with the reality of our days as the beginning point and hope as the future destination. This journey from here to there will require us to climb mountains yet make our home in the valleys in order to finish well. The following illustration maps the steps and process we will travel in order to walk with the Lord, be fruitful, and have an impact.

There are four mountaintops that have a practical and spiritual connection: **CHAOS**: the storm and hope, **ORDER**: surrender and stewardship, **MATURITY**: contentment and generosity, and **ETERNITY**: ministry and kingdom.

There are also four major valleys we can live in and move through that will promote our growth and ability to flourish: **RECONCILE, ESTABLISH, SACRIFICE, TAKE ACTION.**

We need perspective to move from one mountaintop to the next, yet life is not lived on top of mountains. Life is lived in the valleys. We can look at this two ways:

1. Valleys are the low points where difficulties abound, and
2. Valleys are where one grows crops, finds streams of fresh water, and finds refuge in the storms. If we are going to live in contentment we need to accept, be at peace, and even enjoy living in the valleys, because that is where we, too, grow and find the presence of the Lord.

The challenge is that we can't live on the mountaintops as the weather is harsh and there is little water and vegetation. These mountaintops are hurdles or hallmarks of our actions that reflect spiritual growth and the practical living out of the Christian life.

As you look at the picture you will see the four mountains, which form the acronym COME and represent four different calls the Lord make for us to come. The four valleys make the acronym REST. We are to answer the Call to "COME" and "REST" as in Matthew 11:28-30, *"Come to Me, all who are weary and heavy-laden, and I will give you Rest. Take My yoke upon you and learn from Me, for I am gentle and humble in heart, and you will find rest for your souls. For My yoke is easy and My burden is light."*

4 MOUNTAINS = 4 Calls to COME; Come... take up his Cross – Luke 9:23 ; Come to Me and Drink – John 7:37-38; Come I will make you fishers of men – Matthew 4:19; Jesus said, "If you wish to be complete, go and sell your possessions and give to the poor, and you will have treasure in heaven; and come, follow Me." Matthew 19:21

4 VALLEYS = 4 REST Areas; Reconcile – 2 Corinthians 5:20; Establish – Colossians 2:6-7; Sacrifice – Romans 12:1-2; Tenacity – Hebrews 11; Grow and Heal – be made whole

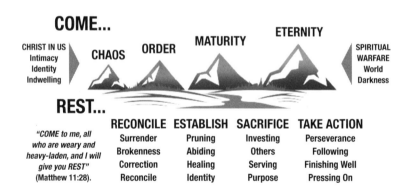

We also note that that with each mountain there are levels of fruit as the outcome. These reflect the four levels of fruit found in John 15:1-16: **No Fruit** (vs 2a), **Fruit** (vs 2b), **More/Much Fruit** (vs 2-5), **Multiplying Fruit** (vs 16).

1 "I am the true vine, and My Father is the vinedresser. 2 Every branch in Me that does not bear fruit, He takes away; and every branch that bears fruit, He prunes it so that it may bear more fruit. 3 You are already clean because of the word which I have spoken to you. 4 Abide in Me, and I in you. As the branch cannot bear fruit of itself unless it abides in the vine, so neither can you unless you abide in Me. 5 I am the vine, you are the branches; he who abides in Me and I in him, he bears much fruit, for apart from Me you can do nothing...."

13 "Greater love has no one than this, that one lay down his life for his friends. ...16 You did not choose Me but I chose you, and appointed you that you would go and bear fruit, and that your fruit would remain, so that whatever you ask of the Father in My name He may give to you."

Mountain	Key Descriptor	Levels of Fruit
CHAOS	Wilderness	No Fruit (vs 2a)
ORDER	Common Sense	Fruit (vs 2b)
MATURITY	Wisdom	More/Much Fruit (vs 2-5)
ETERNITY	The Kingdom	Multiplying Fruit (vs 16)

As you reflect on this mountain and valley analogy, assess yourself. Where are you? Actually it is quite insightful to examine yourself in four areas: Money, Work, Relationships, and Walk with the Lord.

We see in this illustration that the long-term goal of the Lord is transformation of who we are (identity that translates into action) and that we would become followers and not just raving fans in some stadium cheering on Jesus.

The final goal in this journey is to leave a legacy of changed lives (much and multiplying fruit). We will realize this when our hope is found in Jesus Christ and He works through our weaknesses. We will also come to understand that where our treasure is there our heart will be also and this world is not our home.

LEARN TO RESPOND WELL

For us to finish well and enter into the joy of our Master we need to respond well to both the good and the challenges of life. Here are seven ways we can practice responding well:

1. Thank the Lord always in prayer. Also seek the Lord's guidance.
2. Take Responsibility where you are. Own the situation and embrace the pain. Don't miss the lesson.
3. Remember you are not alone. Learn to rest in the Spirit.
4. Put on the mind of Christ. Don't rely on your emotions.
5. Don't blame God, others or self for the difficulties. Learn from them.
6. Step out in faith. Do the NEXT, BEST, RIGHT thing.
7. As a result of the valley and even while in it, seek to help others. The ministry of the Lord flows through you as you set your mind on others.

LIFE IN THE VALLEY

This illustration reveals successive and deeper levels of surrender required in order to move to ever deepening levels in and intimate heart relationship with the Lord. These are "the valleys" where we live and it is *not easy*. Valleys are known for a level of difficulty and pain. Yet valleys are good in that this is where you find water and food and plants grow, and there is some protection from the storms of life. Fruit is borne in the valleys. So life in the valley is a process that brings both good and hardship or surrender. Those levels of surrender are:

- **Repentance and Brokenness** – We need to repent and change course by seeking the Lord and His Word.
- **Pruning and Abiding** – This is marked by "Faithful Obedience." We need to be trustworthy and put into practice Christ's teaching.
- **Sacrificing and Investing** – We give our lives and possessions to help others. We live by surrendering our possessions on behalf of others.

- **Persevering and Following** – Our lives display Christ as our life. We surrender our whole life.

Being able to live in the valley is at the heart of being content. When we make the best of where the Lord has placed us, we learn, improve, and move to a deeper level of spiritual intimacy and fruitfulness. This is at the heart of "flourishing," yet it takes time and faithfulness. Our end goal is to hear the Lord say to us, "Well done. good and faithful servant."

Here is a summary of the four valleys, their key descriptors, and characteristics of each place:

Valley	Key Descriptor	Characteristics
RECONCILE	Death	Correction, chastisement/repent
ESTABLISH	Dependence	Pruning, abiding, persevere/intimacy
SACRIFICE	Others	Investing, serving, ministry/love
TAKE ACTION	Faithfulness	Persevere, well done faithful servant

TWO SIDES OF THE MOUNTAIN – *CHAOS*

There are two types of people who journey and camp out on the Mountain of **CHAOS**. They are the pre-Christian and the Baby Christian. These people have totally different hearts, yet outwardly are very similar in that they tend to be still focused on themselves and their needs. They make rather poor judgments in relationships and in the practical use of finances. Their lives are marked by many ups and downs emotionally, mentally, and spiritually. The have more than their fair share of challenges because they tend not to make great choices. There is little to no fruit in the spiritual lives.

Many people like to stay here because it is filled with fun, games, and entertainment that can outweigh or medicate the pain. It is only when the pain and its consequences become too unbearable that people consider making choices that lead to correction and a change of course. Correction and change is the only path to **ORDER** and one must climb that mountain before they can get to maturity.

ORDER

The Mountain of **ORDER** has two sides: ongoing surrender while going up and stewardship on the descent. Climbing the slope of surrender begins with a heart change that puts God in control of the process and results. People must make a Lordship decision. This is a difficult ascent where each successive step can be harder and it is easy to slip backwards. Climbers will need the support of other climbers, learn good climbing techniques, exercise discipline and utilize good equipment. There is a satisfaction as well as a sense of peace and freedom when this side of the mountain is mastered.

The downslope is that of stewardship—the practical giving up of my ownership and control of finances, times, talent, etc. This side of the journey requires an equal amount of discipline, as it is also easy to slip and fall. Journeying on the Mountain of **ORDER** takes faith. We can't see around the next corner; we simply must trust our guide. This part of the trip is rewarding and yields an initial level of fruit.

On the Mountain of **ORDER** people begin to grow and think for themselves. They are able to function on their own and grow spiritually. At this location, people love their peace and freedom, yet in many cases they are still focused on their own worlds—what they need, want, and desire. Peace and freedom can be a barrier to growth. People often feel like those are the goal, while in reality they are only a step along the way.

MATURITY

The Mountain of **MATURITY** reflects a journey that is more about the heart relationships and reflects inner values rather than the activity associated with the Mountain of **ORDER**. The upslope of **MATURITY** is that of contentment, in other words being satisfied with what you have rather always pursing something more. Contentment is learned and marked by being satisfied with the Lord, His presence, and His gifts. Simplicity of life helps one live out this freedom. Contentment settles us on the inside so we can turn our attention, gifts and resources to others.

Generosity is a key mark of **MATURITY**; we are no longer consumed with filling our perceived needs, but we focus on others. Generosity is not just for the affluent; it is a virtue for every individual because it is a generous gift given by the Lord to everyone. We see how generous God is with us, so we want to be generous with others. The Mountain of **MATURITY** demonstrates *love* to others and to the Lord.

To move from **ORDER** to **MATURITY** one undergoes pruning and abiding in the Valley of **ESTABLISH**. We are shaped through adversity to bear more fruit, and it is in abiding with the Lord and entering into a deeper love relationship with Him that we bear much fruit. **MATURITY** with its characteristics of contentment and generosity is not the end goal of the Christian journey. It is a stop over, a place to enjoy, yet not the end.

ETERNITY

Our journey carries on to the Mountain of **ETERNITY** where the Lord is glorified, the world is impacted, and we are fulfilled. The two sides to this mountain consist of ministry and Kingdom focus. Ministry is that place where we have already gone through the valley of investing and sacrificing our lives and our resources, so now the focus is sharing the gospel and helping others walk with the Lord. It is a whole-life investment. The backside of eternity is the Kingdom, which is also our destination of *hope*.

We are called to seek first the Kingdom of God and all these things will be added to us. The blessing of the Mountain of **ETERNITY** is that now others who we have helped begin to bear fruit and start on their own journeys. We leave a legacy of multiplying fruit.

This mountain will not be without difficulty and struggle, because the spiritual battle will intensify; you will have a mark on your back that the enemy wants to go after. We are called to stand against the rulers and forces of darkness while we continue to follow the Lord. Our reward will be the sound of "Well done, good and faithful servant, enter into the joy of your master" (see Matthew 25:21).

Mountain – Stage	Two Sides of the Mountain	Heart Attitudes & Outcome	Fruit Level Characteristics
CHAOS – Baby	Pre-Christian – Selfish, self-centered, issues and problems abound	PAIN >> CHOICES We have pain and begin to see the need for and actually begin to make some wise choices. It is hard to live in Chaos ongoing.	No Fruit Chaos is marked by SELF and all of the struggles and difficulties associated with it.
	Baby Christian – Committed to Christ, yet still infant in heart issues, need a lot of support, problems still exist. Need help.		
ORDER – Child	Surrender – The Lord is on the throne and we are daily dying to the flesh. First "Lifestyle Choice"	DISCIPLINE >> PEACE & FREEDOM Choices become discipline and obedience. We exercise the spiritual disciplines: Prayer, Word, Silence, Solitude Exercise Wisdom.	Fruit – some fruit is beginning to be seen. Order is a stage of choosing to walk by FAITH. We are confronted with the pull of the world and the things of the Lord.
	Stewardship – God is owner and we are managers of time, talent, treasure, truth, relationships, gospel		
MATURITY – Young Adult	Contentment – My life does not consist of possessions, power, or position. Marked by satisfaction and simplicity.	COMMITMENT>> SERVING Faithful obedience and discipline leads to commitment and serving others. Our Purpose becomes clarified.	Through pruning and abiding we bear More Fruit & Much Fruit. Maturity is marked by LOVE. We love the Lord and people and not the things of the world.
	Generosity – Become other centered and have great joy in giving away bountifully		
ETERNITY – Adult	Ministry – Begin to invest all resources to help others grow and reproduce.	PRESSING ON >> STAND Life is marked by pressing on in spite of challenges, pressing into the Lord, and standing firm against the enemy. This world is not our home.	As we invest in people they begin to bear Fruit that multiplies. We gain an eternal HOPE that is Kingdom and Christ focused.
	Kingdom – God is glorified, people are changed, and we are fulfilled		

TEN OBSERVATIONS

1. Climbing mountains and living in the valleys is a journey and process that is not linear. It is often two steps forward and one step back. It has pitfalls and many ditches. Our lives should be marked by direction, not perfection. Progress will come from the life and strength of Christ compelling us forward, not just our sheer effort, knowledge, and skills. It is a spiritual journey of growth in a real world of challenge. Our attitudes and actions towards finances are excellent indicators of where we are on our journey.

2. This journey is not about speed or arriving first. We don't truly arrive until we breathe our last and see the face of the Lord. Thus the journey is more about faithfulness and perseverance than the pace. In fact we need to enjoy the moment and seize each day as if it were our last. Age does not mean progress; one can live as a one-year-old thirty times over.

3. Life on top of the mountains offers perspective, we see where we have come from and where we are going. Life at the top can be cool and refreshing, yet offers little sustenance of water or food. The elements can be harsh and one is more exposed to them at this place.

4. Living in the valleys is marked by both good and difficulty. The good is that is where the water is, the plants and fruit is raised as well as other people live. We have protection from the storms of life. Yet the valleys also represent hard choices of surrender and giving up if we are to move forward.

5. Each mountain and each valley represent different stages and maturity levels of life, and that includes our spiritual life. We are called to grow up and not live like children the rest of our days. We can move forward and backward from one stage to another due to unwise choices and the spiritual battle.

6. One can't make this journey alone. It takes support, care, love, nurture of one another to progress. We need community. There are different needs at each level that we need to be aware of.

7. The mountains and valleys don't define who we are. They do shape and allow us to grow into who we are from God's perspective.

8. Because we are complex people with many facets (relationships, finances, work, purpose, emotions), we can be at two different places at the same time. We can have maturity in relationships and chaos in finances. This will bring more challenges, so each one needs a high level of reflection to observe where they are and how to move forward.

9. We will discover that we are never truly at home on this journey. We are made for a home in heaven, and we are aliens passing through this life. We are being prepared for heaven by how we walk in this world.

10. The attitudes of thankfulness, gratefulness, humility, being others centered, and spiritually thirsty will help us in every stage of this journey.

The Lord allows us to walk through the valley. In fact, much of life is lived there, so we will see Him and grow in relationship with Him because we need Him. If we were always on top and doing well, we would most likely forget the Lord and think too highly of ourselves. In the valley we will be a help to fellow strugglers on the journey of life with us. Finally, in the valley we find we will need God's guidance in order to follow His purposes. The pursuit of God's purposes gives us a motivation far greater than the pursuit of this world's goods. They are trinkets and toys compared to the riches of Christ.

Many wander through life without a purpose, not knowing what they are supposed to be doing. Those people find themselves unhappy most of their lives because they don't enjoy what they do and because they lack a purpose. Or they know what they should do and are afraid of doing it because of all the "what ifs" and the false expectations that appear to be real.

Consider the words of A. W. Tozer:

"In back of every wasted life is a bad philosophy, an erroneous conception of life's worth and purpose. The man who believes that he was born to get all he can will spend his life trying to get it. The man who believes he was created to enjoy fleshly pleasures will devote himself to pleasure seeking; and if by a combination of favorable circumstance he manages to get a lot of fun out of life, his pleasures will all turn to ashes in his mouth at the last. He will find out too late that God made him too noble to be satisfied with those tawdry pleasures he had devoted his life to here under the sun."

APPLICATIONS

1. Keep your eyes open, learn where you are and be a student of how to move forward.
2. Assess and reflect where you are.
3. Seek wisdom and guidance from fellow travelers. You can't go alone.
4. Embrace the journey; enjoy each day and each relationship.
5. Accept the pains and difficulties as stepping stones and a means of growing.
6. Be willing to take risks of faith, make deposits of life, and keep your hope alive.

NEXT STEPS OF OUR JOURNEY

We are called to embrace the journey. Each of us are on a journey of growing in our walk with the Lord, being conformed to His image, becoming mature and giving our lives away. These journeys are both very unique and yet have similarities to the hurdles and difficulties we will face. Having a picture or map of the journey gives us perspective as well as helps us navigate the ups and downs along the way. We also can anticipate what lies ahead so we are not caught unaware. Each journey has the same destination of **HOME**, which is an eternal life in heaven with the Lord and His saints. We climb the mountains and yet live in the valleys. The following chart summarizes each of the mountains and valleys.

COME	Chaos	Order	Maturity	Eternity	Victory, Flourish, Triumph, Overcome, Success, Thrive, Abundance, Prosper
4 Calls to Come: Mt 11:28-30 Lu 9:23 Jn 7:37-38 Mt 4:18	Empty, Self-Focus, Entangles, Busy, Barren, Division, Brokenness, Despair, No Hope – No Fruit, Entertainment, Fun, Distraction, Baby	Preparation, Fruit, Stewardship, Engaged, Peace, Freedom, Child, Delayed Gratification	God's Will, Purpose, More/Much Fruit, Calling, Release, Abundance, Contentment, Generosity, Wisdom, Character, Walk Worthy,	Faithfulness, Fulfillment, Convergence, Overflow, Multiplying Fruit, Kingdom Impact	
REST	**Reconcile (Surrender)**	**Establish**	**Sacrifice**	**Take Action**	Hope, Finish Well, Living Well, Heaven, True Home
Mt 11:28-30 Heb 4	Valley of Repentance, Valley of Dependence, Correction, Die to Self, Pain	Valley of Pruning, Abiding, Growth, Molded, Intimacy, Identity, Indwelling, Wholeness, Wait on the Lord, Comfort, Healing	Valley of Others, Community, Significance, Invest	Valley of Pressing In/ Pressing On Valley of Perseverance	

KNOW THAT THE PROCESS IS THE END – APPLICATION

1. Assess yourself Spiritually, Relationally, and Vocationally.
2. Have a personal development plan and engage with others. (Accountability and small group)

REMEMBER THESE THREE CONSTANT FACTORS

1. God is on the throne and in control. He is good and has our best interests always at heart. We have hope.

2. Satan is alive and on the warpath against us. He is always seeking to kill, steal, and destroy. The days are evil.

3. Every believer has "the gift"—intimacy marked by the unconditional love from God, identity which is being a new person "in Christ" and indwelling which is the Spirit and life of Christ residing in them. It is our hope that leads to faith.

WE ARE CALLED TO APPROPRIATE CHRIST

The variable for each of us is how we live this "Christ Life." Are we faithful and obedient? Do we seek His will and Kingdom above our desires, are we serving others, have we given up ownership and become stewards of the time, talent, treasure, truth, relationships, and grace that has been given us? Are we loving God, self and others? What is our perspective of the trials and our true home? These are a few of the questions we will encounter.

Appropriating Christ in us is the critical factor at each stage of life we encounter. He has given us eternal life, given us everything that pertains to life and godliness. He is our hope and strength. Appropriation is taking hold and living by the means (love, grace, strength, relationships, etc.) that Christ has given to us. Appropriation is by faith, discipline, applying His Word and growing up in Him. This growth is found as we journey through the stages of our mountains and valleys and as we make decisions to apply the 7 Secrets of an Abundant Journey.

We are promised that we will have and experience an abundant life—life filled with Christ, the fruit of the spirit, grace, and hope. That being said, it is not a life without challenges, hurt, pain, and difficulty. This is the picture of the journey that each of us are on.

In the following chapters, we will examine more in depth each of mountains and valleys to understand what happens there and how we progress.

Chapter 7

THE MOUNTAIN OF CHAOS

"Wake Up and Own It"
KEY DESCRIPTOR: Wilderness
CHARACTERISTICS: Self and Emptiness

The Mountain for **CHAOS** is a wilderness, a place of self and sin. This mountain begins with all of the glitter and glitz of the world, filled with fun and pleasure, yet it only leads to misery, destruction and despair. Consider the following verses to put a biblical perspective to the mountain.

> *"'Beware, and be on your guard against every form of greed; for not even when one has an abundance does his life consist of his possessions.' And He told them a parable, saying, 'The land of a rich man was very productive. And he began reasoning to himself, saying, '"What shall I do, since I have no place to store my crops?" Then he said, "This is what I will do: I will tear down my barns and build larger ones, and there I will store all my grain and my goods. And I will say to my soul, 'Soul, you have many goods laid up for many years to come; take your ease, eat, drink and be merry.'" But God said to him, "You fool! This very night your soul is required of you; and now who will own what you have prepared?" So is the man who stores up treasure for himself, and is not rich toward God'"* (Luke 12:15-21).

"So also we, while we were children, were held in bondage under the elemental things of the world" (Galatians 4:3).

CHAOS UNPACKED

We all begin in chaos because we really don't know any better. We can learn by the school of hard knocks, from others, and from the Lord. There are many ways to describe chaos, but the best picture is that of a baby or toddler: Someone who is needy, focused on self, does not know how to give, and loves to be entertained in order to be happy. Underneath the surface, chaos is marked by hurt, pain, aloneness, unknowns, selfishness, sin, busyness, fixation on entertainment, being pain free, division, broken relationships, immaturity, and damaged emotions. There is a constant pursuit of possessions, power, pleasure, or entertainment. Chaos is destructive to self and others, always desiring to center on the moment with no vision of the future or learning from the past. It is very empty and never satisfies long term.

None of us have all of these attributes or descriptions, yet any one of them can take us to the sidelines. This stage frames our start but not our finish. Challenges and difficulties are not necessarily chaos. They can be a consequence of chaos. They also can be no fault of our own actions (actually a result of going against the world). The Lord can use them to grow and move us in the direction of maturity.

The critical factor of being in chaos is to wake up! We need to realize we are nowhere and going nowhere. This wake-up call may come in many forms: hurt, pain, loss; but, it is enough to grab our attention. Once awake, we need to take responsibility for our own actions and attitudes. We own up to whatever our part is and then deal with the consequences. Blaming others or being in denial are hallmarks of being in a state of chaos.

The truth in this verse, *"Where your treasure is, there your heart will be also"* (Matthew 6:21) helps us understand if we are in chaos or not. Just consider what you truly treasure, what brings you value and pleasure. This then is an indication of where our hearts are. If we primarily treasure fun, entertainment, self-orientation, and worldly desires, then it is fairly certain we are in a state of chaos or will soon be. If, on the other hand, we pursue the things of the Lord, people, the Word, then we are at a much different place in the journey.

Chaos and Resources

Chaos as it relates to finances and resources is marked by a sense of ownership, pleasing myself, immediate gratification, hoarding, spending out of control, and being in debt, just to name a few. The consequences of these are bondage, despair, relational struggles, and a sense of hopelessness. Chaos is also marked by inconsistency, squandering what we do manage, having little sense of self-restraint, and a lack of faithfulness. We can't be trusted to do what we say. Our only commitment is to self, not others.

Chaos and Relationships

Chaos can also hit us in our relationships: marriage, family, or personal. This is marked by pure selfishness, getting our needs met before others, or simply being self-serving and using people. From here the outcome is to dictate, manipulate, whine, or attack. When we are in chaos relationally, our hurts go unhealed and we grow in fear and anger, which escalate to bitterness and despair. We don't resolve our hurts; we bury them or try to ignore them.

One way this manifests itself is a focus on my needs and the other person's lack of character rather then reflecting on my own character and how I could serve the other person's needs. Childishness in relationships is marked by either an over-focus on rules rather than grace in relationships or busyness with no clear sense of purpose.

Another picture of this stage is when our relationships are just surface with no vulnerability and authenticity. It is a sense of pseudo-community. This is also marked by the tendency to live out of our emotions and feelings.

Chaos is Where We Begin

We all begin in chaos. It is a land of make-believe, we think things are well on the surface, but our lives and relationships are rotting under the surface. The characteristics we outlined above frame our start but not our finish. We must learn our lesson, because if we don't, we will go around the mountain again.

SUMMARY

In Chaos, wake up and own it. Mountain of Wilderness (Self & Emptiness)

Don't Blame or Deny

We all begin in chaos that is marked by hurt, pain, aloneness, unknowns, selfishness, sin, busyness, fixation on entertainment, being pain free, division, broken relationships, immaturity, and damaged emotions. There is a constant pursuit of possessions, power, pleasure, or entertainment. We don't have all of these, yet any one can take us to the sidelines. They frame our start but not our finish.

- **Step 1 – Wake up.** Assess your actions, attitudes, behaviors. Be honest with yourself; no one is perfect. We all can grow.
- **Step 2 – Own your issues.** The Lord knows where you are. Embrace it no matter whose fault. Don't blame others.
- **Step 3 – Believe change is possible.** There is no limit as to what could happen. Challenge yourself to think and be different.
- **Step 4 – Plant seeds of hope.** Don't give up. Begin with Christ in you as the hope of glory. (See Colossians 1:27.)

Where your treasure is your heart will be also.
(See Matthew 6:19-21.)

Chapter 8

THE VALLEY OF RECONCILE

"Surrender Is the First Step to Victory"
KEY DESCRIPTOR: Wilderness
CHARACTERISTICS: Brokenness and Pain

"Childlike surrender and trust, I believe, is the defining spirit of authentic discipleship."

– Brennan Manning

"We can only learn to know ourselves and do what we can—namely, surrender our will and fulfill God's will in us."

– Saint Teresa of Avila

"Surrendering means giving something over to God then replacing it with something from Him."

– Kevin Martineau

In the journey to move one from the Mountain of **CHAOS** to the Mountain of **ORDER**, we all have to go through the Valley of **RECONCILE** filled with brokenness and pain. This takes a process of surrender and stewardship. Surrender is the willful giving up of the control and results of our lives and allows the Lord to rule and reign. This is the first step to having victory, although we never sign up for it. Surrender is measured by our faithfulness and is marked by the Lord working in and through us. If we are faithful, we will be given the true riches—eternal riches. We also note that we can only pursue and serve one master—either the Lord or worldly resources. The choice is ours. The spiritual aspect of this is surrender, and the practical side is how we steward our finances. This begins to put us on the road to order and bearing fruit.

So we will begin with Jesus' story of the unrighteous steward found in Luke 16:1-13.

> *"Now He was also saying to the disciples, "There was a rich man who had a manager, and this manager was reported to him as squandering his possessions. And he called him and said to him, 'What is this I hear about you? Give an accounting of your management, for you can no longer be manager.' The manager said to himself, 'What shall I do, since my master is taking the management away from me? I am not strong enough to dig; I am ashamed to beg. I know what I shall do, so that when I am removed from the management people will welcome me into their homes.' And he summoned each one of his master's debtors, and he began saying to the first, 'How much do you owe my master?' And he said, 'A hundred measures of oil.' And he said to him, 'Take your bill, and sit down quickly and write fifty.' Then he said to another, 'And how much do you owe?' And he said, 'A hundred measures of wheat.' He said to him, 'Take your bill, and write eighty.' And his master praised the unrighteous manager because he had acted shrewdly; for the sons of this age are more shrewd in relation to their own kind than the sons of light. And I say to you, make friends for yourselves by means of the wealth of unrighteousness, so that when it fails, they will receive you into the eternal dwellings.*
>
> *"He who is faithful in a very little thing is faithful also in much; and he who is unrighteous in a very little thing is unrighteous also in much. Therefore if you have not been faithful in the use of unrighteous wealth, who will entrust the true riches*

to you? And if you have not been faithful in the use of that which is another's, who will give you that which is your own? No servant can serve two masters; for either he will hate the one and love the other, or else he will be devoted to one and despise the other. You cannot serve God and wealth."

What are the lessons from this parable? Several are key: stewardship or our handling of resources is measured and reflected by faithfulness. The Lord gives us resources to test and see just how faithful are we—a little or much? Our faithfulness will have a reward.

The next lesson is "who is our master—the Lord or our wealth?" Jesus states that we will have only one master. This is also found in Matthew 6:24, *"No one can serve two masters. Either you will hate the one and love the other, or you will be devoted to the one and despise the other. You cannot serve both God and money"* (NIV). The question becomes which is your master? Who or what owns us—God or money? Interestingly, the word money here actually is the word *mammon*, which is an evil force associated with money but far more powerful. This mammon can grip us and control our thoughts and attitudes.

The choice is ours. To whom do we submit and surrender the heart? We will choose either the Lord or money. The nature of that surrender is all encompassing. We don't half surrender—it is all or nothing. This surrender involves all of our choices, because when we surrender, we give up control. This surrender of the heart can be further examined by six lifestyle choices that each of us must make if we are to follow the Lord with a whole heart.

6 LIFESTYLE CHOICES

NATURE	CHOICE	VERSE	QUESTION
Personal	Decease or Increase	John 3:30	Who is first?
Strength	Weak or Strong	2 Corinthians 12:9-11	Can we overcome any obstacle?
Power	Received or Achieved	John 15:5	Who is the source of power?
Relationships	Give or Take	Acts 20:35	Who do I help?
Material	Possess or Let Go	Matthew 6:24	Who or what is the master?
Process	Entitled or Faithful	Luke 16:12	How are you doing?

Choices are reflective of our character. The nature of a godly character in our lives is to have an obedient heart—choosing to follow the Lord above all else. It is a desire to *be* pleasing to God and to *do* the will of God in all things. This requires being broken rather than being proud. The chart below gives us insight into the heart condition of these two kinds of people. These choices begin with relinquishing our pride and embracing our brokenness.

PROUD PEOPLE	BROKEN PEOPLE
Focus on the failure of others	Overwhelmed with a sense of their own spiritual need
A critical, fault-finding spirit; looking at everyone else's faults with a microscope, but their own with a telescope	Compassionate; can forgive much because they know how much they have been forgiven
Self-righteous; look down on others	Esteem all others better than themselves
Independent, self-sufficient spirit	Have a dependent spirit; recognize a need for others
Have to prove they are right; Claim rights; have a demanding spirit	Willing to yield the right to be right
Self-protective of their time, their rights and their reputation	Self-denying
Desire to be served	Motivated to serve others

John 12:24 provides us with a promise that ties being fruitful and flourishing to being broken and surrendered: *"Truly, truly, I say to you, unless a grain of wheat falls into the earth and dies, it remains alone; but if it dies, it bears much fruit."* Surrender and choosing to put the Lord in control is much easier said than done, and it is a daily choice which is seen in Luke 9:23, *"And He was saying to them all, "If anyone wishes to come after Me, he must deny himself, and take up his cross daily and follow Me."* See the chart below comparing the proud and the broken.

We who know Christ are called to surrender our will unconditionally to the Lord. God, however, has given us the freedom to choose whether to surrender. Unlike the vanquished in war, our decision to surrender is motivated by the Lord's unconditional love for us, not that we are a defeated foe. Our surrender is an act of worship. *"Therefore, I urge you, brothers, in view of God's mercy, to offer your bodies as living sacrifices, holy and pleasing to God—this is your spiritual act of worship"* (Romans 12:1 NIV).

Charles Spurgeon's primary qualification for serving God with any degree of success and for doing His work well and triumphantly was a sense of our own weakness:

> *"When the Lord's warrior marches forth to battle, strong in his own might or when he boasts, "I know I will be victorious, for my own mighty arm and conquering sword will give me the victory," defeat is not far away. God will not go forward with the person who marches ahead in his own strength. He who counted on victory in this fashion has counted wrongly, for "Not by might nor by power, but by my Spirit,' says the Lord Almighty" (Zechariah 4:6). Those who enter the battle boasting of their own process will return with their victory banners dragging through the dust and their armor stained with disgrace.*
>
> *"God will empty you of yourself before He will put His resources in you, cleaning out your granary before filling it with the finest of his wheat. The river of the Lord is full of water, but not one drop of it flows from earthly springs. He will never allow any strength to be used in His battles except that which He Himself imparts.*
>
> *"Believer, are you mourning your own weakness? Take courage, for you must have an awareness of your own weakness before the Lord will give you victory. Your emptiness is the necessary preparation for being filled, and being cast down is simply preparing you to be lifted up."*

MANY FACETS OF SURRENDER

When we use the term *surrender* it can have many synonyms, descriptions, and postures biblically: broken, repent, give up, or conform. These various postures reveal principles that lead to processes at work resulting in God producing His outcomes. Review the chart below and reflect on the bigger picture of surrender and how God uses it in our individual lives and to advance His Kingdom purposes.

SURRENDER			
Posture – Description	Principle – Cause or action to be taken	Process – God at work	Product – Outcome
Yielded Repentance	Surrender is a choice	Hope is clarified	Blessing comes from giving up
Conformed	Acknowledge and	Faith is built	New life from dying
Broken	repent from sin	Clean conduits	Releases the power
Humbled	God disciplines	Priorities reduced	of Christ
Persecuted	those He loves	Molds our character	We can hear the
Transformed	(chastises)	Develops purity	Lord
Sacrifice	Take up your cross	Creates dependence	We "know" the Lord
Weakness	daily	Brings humility	Witness to the world
Decrease	Dying to self	Enhances need for	Hope to a lost world
Let go of control	Brokenness and	others	Defeats the enemy
Give Up	pain due to self	Value one another	Builds community
Every knee will	Hurt and loss	Become available	Multiplies the
bow	caused by others	Obedience grows	church
Slave/servant	Spiritual Battle with	Experience comfort	Grows our ministry
Steward	World, Flesh, &	Stand in face of	Allows God to show
Die to self	Devil	Tyranny	up
Abandon	Emotional hurt	God's way is higher	Brings Revival
Empty	in relationships	than ours	Abiding comes out
At the end of	Persecution and	Be still and be at	of rest
myself	rejection	rest	Refueling our soul
	Trials and Struggles	Listen to God	Paradoxes are
	Worn out and spent	speaking	realized (weak to be
	God's ways and	Can only fill an	strong; dying to live;
	thoughts are not	empty cup	giving to receive)
	ours		
	Course correction,		
	Choose a new path		
	Stop the activity –		
	be still, be at rest		
	Disease and		
	sickness		
	Wars, rumors of		
	war/great destruction		
	God shouts to us in		
	our pain		
	Believing God has		
	my best interests at		
	heart		

JESUS CHRIST MODELED SURRENDER

In the life of Christ, we see that He completely humbled and submitted himself to His Heavenly Father, so that God was free to work powerfully through Him. Here are some examples of Christ humbling Himself to His Father. Note how Jesus used the words nothing when referring to Himself.

- *"The Son can do nothing of Himself"* (John 5:19).
- *"I [Jesus] can do nothing on My own initiative. As I hear, I judge; and My judgment is just, because I do not seek My own will, but the will of Him who sent Me"* (John 5:30).

ARE YOU WILLING TO SURRENDER?

Jesus was willing to surrender to God, and He tells us to do likewise, *"And he who does not take his cross and follow after Me is not worthy of Me. He who has found his life will lose it, and he who has lost his life for My sake will find it"* (Matthew 10:38-39).

It requires nothing less than a transformation of our hearts to submit to Christ as Lord, as our Life, and as the Leader. Because of our own pride and the world's perspective of being in control that is so deeply ingrained in most of us, it can require years and often difficult circumstances to completely humble ourselves and embrace God's way of life.

In the 1600s, Francois Fenelon wrote a letter to his friends in prison that capture this understanding:

> *"And the very proof that God loves you is that He does not spare you, but lays upon you the cross of Jesus Christ. Whatever spiritual knowledge or feelings we may have, they are all a delusion if they do not lead us to the real and constant practice of dying to self. And it is true that we do not die without suffering. Nor is it possible to be considered truly dead while there is any part of us which is yet alive.*
>
> *"This spiritual death (which is really a blessing in disguise) is undeniably painful. It cuts 'swift and deep into our innermost*

thoughts and desires with all their parts, exposing us for what we really are.' The great Physician, who sees in us what we cannot see, knows exactly where to place the knife. He cuts away that which we are most reluctant to give up. And how it hurts! But we must remember that pain is only felt where there is life, and where there is life is just the place where death is needed."

LETTING LOOSE OF CONTROL AND RESULTS

One of the great enemies of spiritual growth and flourishing is the craving to control our environment and the desire to determine the results of our endeavors. We cannot be responsive to God's purposes until we abandon our strategies to control and acknowledge His exclusive owner-ship of our lives. Many of us have a natural inclination to be manipulators, grabbers, owners, and controllers. The more we seek to rule our world, the more we will resist the rule of Christ; those who grasp are afraid of being grasped by God. But until we relinquish ownership of our lives, we will not experience the relief of surrender to God's good purposes.

Dr. Ken Boa reinforces this thought:

"Our resistance to God's rule even extends to our prayer-ful attempts to persuade the Lord to bless our plans and to meet our needs in the ways we deem best. Instead of seeking God's will in prayer, we hope to induce Him to accomplish our will. Thus, even in our prayers, we can adopt the mentality of a consumer rather than a servant. We have little control over opportunities we encounter and the outcomes of our efforts, but we can be obedient to the process."

OUR ATTITUDE – THANKFULNESS

We have concluded we are not in control of the results and circumstances of our lives, yet we do exercise a level of control of how we "play our cards." Do we exercise faithfulness? Can God and others count on our being trustworthy. The second element is our attitude. Are we thankful in all situations whether good or bad? Paul instructs us, *"In everything give thanks; for this is God's will for you in Christ Jesus"* (1 Thessalonians 5:18). Thankfulness is a major hallmark for a Christian and is one of the most practical, simple of the disciplines.

> *"You will be enriched in everything for all liberality, which through us is producing thanksgiving to God"* (2 Corinthians 9:11).

> *"Be anxious for nothing, but in everything by prayer and supplication with thanksgiving let your requests be made known to God"* (Philippians 4:6).

> *"Devote yourselves to prayer, keeping alert in it with an attitude of thanksgiving"* (Colossians 4:2).

> *"But thanks be to God, who always leads us in triumph in Christ, and manifests through us the sweet aroma of the knowledge of Him in every place"* (2 Corinthians 2:14).

> *"For all things are for your sakes, so that the grace which is spreading to more and more people may cause the giving of thanks to abound to the glory of God"* (2 Corinthians 4:15).

The following quotation is from *Cries of the Heart: bringing God near when He feels so far* by Ravi Zacharias:

> *"I think, for example, of the powerful testimony of a woman named Annie Johnston Flint. She was one who lived most of her life in pain. Orphaned early in life, her body was embar-*

rassed by incontinence, weakened by cancer, and twisted and deformed by rheumatoid arthritis. She was incapacitated for so long that according to one eyewitness she needed seven or eight pillows around her body just to cushion the raw sores she suffered from being bedridden. Yet her autobiography is rightly called The Making of the Beautiful. Almost like a minstrel from heaven she penned words that touch the heart in its despairing moments. One of her best-known poems, put to music, reads:

'He giveth more grace when the burdens grow greater,
He sendeth more strength when the labors increase;
To added affliction, He addeth His mercy,
To multiplied trials His multiplied peace.

'When we have exhausted our store of endurance,
When our strength has failed e're the day is half done,
When we reach the end of our hoarded resources
Our Father's full giving has only begun.

'His love has no limits, His grace has no measure,
His power has no boundary known unto men;
For out of His infinite riches in Jesus
He giveth, and giveth, and giveth again!'"

Seeing only the negative aspects of any situation can cause you to miss opportunities, neglect problems that need to be solved, and fail to take action that would otherwise improve your relationships and quality of life. In fact, studies show that pessimists are more likely to develop chronic illnesses later on in life than optimists. Optimists look for the light at the end of the tunnel. If you've always had a pessimistic worldview, it can be difficult to shift your focus, but it is possible to start seeing the glass as half full, not half empty. In fact you may come to realize that glasses are generally full—it's just that gravity attracts the more dense liquid material towards the bottom.

SUMMARY

To live a life that flourishes, we recognize where we are (reality) and where we want to go (hope). Then we begin with an examination of our heart toward the Lord and in practical terms of how we handle money. We conclude that we must live a surrendered life—one that puts and keeps God on the throne and us serving Him.

> *"Almost every great biblical hero was broken by God through multiple life crises or harsh circumstances designed for that purpose. There is no getting around the reality: even the best of us needs to be broken, fully and completely detached from our dalliance with sin, self, and society.*
>
> *"If you examine the individuals involved in all these instances, you'll see that God does not force us to accept brokenness. He always allows us to choose. But if you are wise, you will discover that you either allow God to use circumstances to wake you and break you, or you may count on continuing to fight Him and suffer.*
>
> *"Most people never realize that brokenness is actually a gift from God that demonstrates His awesome and unyielding love. We typically examine the circumstances designed to guide us from a casual acquaintance to an intense and intimate lover of God and foolishly conclude that they are harmful to our well-being. In reality, they are God's means of bringing us to our knees before Him, in full-on repentance, enabling us to see the truth of who we are, who He is, how we treat Him, and how compassionate He is.*
>
> *"In our culture-aided confusion we focus on the deprivation, sacrifice, pain, suffering, hardship, and persecution that God injects into our experience. We mistakenly assume that once we believe nice things about God and invest a few personal resources in the development of our faith, the appropriate re-*

sponse by our Father should be affirmation, comfort, pleasure, rewards, and happiness."

– George Barna

Surrender is the first step to victory. It is accomplished in the Valley of **RECONCILE**, that place of brokenness and dependence where you repent from sin and the flesh, and receive forgiveness, love and grace from Christ.

When we find ourselves in chaos, we are not to despair for there is a way out. Paul tells us that the Lord leads us in triumph also know as an abundant life or victory. Yet this abundance comes from us coming to the end of our resources (a volitional surrender of our will to the Lord's will) and appropriating Christ's resources—His gifts and promises. When we place our stories into God's bigger story we start on the road to victory. We are motivated by the hope of Christ and eternal life in Him.

The corn of wheat that falls to the ground and dies also grows and becomes productive. Death to the old self is the first step to Christian growth and this principle is found in all the New Testament (Romans 8:13). Death to the sinful nature means to be willfully against the works of the flesh, the mentality, philosophies and damnable superstitions of the world. God says that the flesh must be crucified with its sinful lusts (Galatians 5:24). The as you die to SELF then CHRIST is seen in you! Christ must increase and we must decrease! (John 3:30).

Oswald Chambers speaks directly to this:

THE TEACHING OF ADVERSITY

In the world you will have tribulation; but be of good cheer, I have overcome the world. JOHN 16:33

The typical view of the Christian life is that it means being delivered from all adversity. But it actually means being delivered in adversity, which is something very different. "He who dwells in the secret place of the Most High shall abide under the shadow of the Almighty. No evil shall befall you, nor shall any plague come near your dwelling…" (Psalm 91:1,10)—the place where you are at one with God.

If you are a child of God, you will certainly encounter adversities, but Jesus says you should not be surprised when they come. "In the world you will have tribulation; but be of good cheer, I have overcome the world." He is saying, "There is nothing for you to fear." The same people who refused to talk about their adversities before they were saved often complain and worry after being born again because they have the wrong idea of what it means to live the life of a saint.

God does not give us overcoming life—He gives us life as we overcome. The strain of life is what builds our strength. If there is no strain, there will be no strength. Are you asking God to give you life, liberty, and joy? He cannot, unless you are willing to accept the strain. And once you face the strain, you will immediately get the strength. Overcome your own timidity and take the first step. Then God will give you nourishment—"To him who overcomes I will give to eat from the tree of life…" (Revelation 2:7). If you completely give of yourself physically, you become exhausted. But when you give of yourself spiritually, you get more strength. God never gives us strength for tomorrow, or for the next hour, but only for the strain of the moment. Our temptation is to face adversities from the standpoint of our own common sense. But a saint can "be of good cheer" even when seemingly defeated by adversities, because victory is absurdly impossible to everyone, except God.

     – My Utmost for His Highest Updated Edition

VICTORY IN MOUNTAINS AND VALLEYS

SUMMARY

Surrender is the first step to victory and the only path home. The Valley of **RECONCILE** is the place of Death with its Brokenness and Pain.

Turn/Change/Take Responsibility

Repent from sin and/or flesh. Receive forgiveness, love and grace from Christ.

- **Step 1 – Take full responsibility.** Accept the medicine and the consequences of the chaos. Be willing to pay the price.
- **Step 2 – Change starts with me.** I am fully accountable. Face your fears. Change what you can, accept all else.
- **Step 3 – Die to self.** Stop sin before you start to fix it. Out with the old man/in with the new. Don't fight the wrong battle.
- **Step 4 – Victory believes in a better future and hope.** You are not stuck. Think big. Know Christ can/will work. Don't quit.

To live you must die. Surrender your life to gain Christ's life.
(See Galatians 2:20.)

Chapter 9

THE MOUNTAIN OF ORDER

"Give Up Ownership and Do the Right Things"
KEY DESCRIPTOR: Common Sense
CHARACTERISTICS: Stewardship and Faithfulness

COMMON SENSE REQUIRES GIVING UP OWNERSHIP

We begin our climb of the Mountain of **ORDER** with determining who is on the "throne" of our life and resources. Is it ourselves or the Lord? Order requires us to give up ownership and pursue Christ's Lordship in our lives. As we let go of ownership, we begin operating out of stewardship, things find their proper place in our lives, and we find order. When we are no longer entangled by worldly goods, we are free. We are now stewards (managers), and the Lord is now the owner.

Order occurs as we take practical steps of pursuing the right purposes and priorities defined by the Lord and His Word. Order takes the clutter out of our life and puts the right things in the right places. This is why common sense is the key descriptor for the Mountain of **ORDER**. As you climb this mountain, you are simply doing the right things in the right way. You are learning to function as a good steward, surrendering to God as the true Owner.

GOD IS THE OWNER

In order to put the heart condition of surrender into practice, we need to look at our finances and how we handle money. Our use of money is an outward indicator of our spiritual condition and our walk with the Lord.

So, who owns your money and finances? The world tells us that we do, and our flesh craves for this to be so. Yet biblically the case is just the opposite. Look at who is the owner in this passage: *"Yours, O Lord, is the greatness, the power, the glory, the victory, and the majesty. Everything in the heavens and on earth is yours, O Lord, and this is your kingdom. We adore you as the one who is over all things. Wealth and honor come from you alone, for you rule over everything. Power and might are in your hand, and at your discretion people are made great and given strength"* (1 Chronicles 29:11-12 NLT).

And what does God own? *"The earth is the Lord's, and all it contains, the world, and those who dwell in it"* (Psalm 24:1). Many others verses confirm that God owns all of the world's wealth: the gold, silver, and even the cattle on a thousand hills.

When we view God as the owner, we assume the role of steward or manager. This is where the rubber meets the road. We must give up the ownership of our wealth, finances, and life in practical, tangible ways to pursue a radical lifestyle, serving the Lord. That surrender carries large consequences and implications.

OUT OF SURRENDER COMES OUR ROLE AS FAITHFUL STEWARD

The key verse that describes our role in life and in our finances is 1 Corinthians 4:2, *"Moreover, it is required of stewards that one be found trustworthy"* (RSV). A manager is defined as "a person responsible for and in charge of administering all or part of a company or similar organization that is not their own." Managers have a full level of responsibility and must be trustworthy and skilled to function well. This applies in particular to how we handle our finances. The Lord calls us first to be faithful—someone trustworthy with the wise use of money and resources. Not only does the Lord count on us to be a good manager, our families need us to be faithful stewards also or there will be more chaos in the relationships around us.

Faithfulness is a reflection of our character and is a quality that can be learned and improved. We grow in faithfulness by doing little things well and then we can be entrusted with more. *"He who is faithful in a very little thing is faithful also in much; and he who is unrighteous in a very little thing is unrighteous also in much. Therefore if you have not been faithful in the use of unrighteous wealth, who will entrust the true riches to you? And if you have not been faithful in the use of that which is another's, who will give you that which is your own?"* (Luke 16:10-12).

Dr. Ken Boa speaks on the issue of stewardship and being faithful in *Conformed to His Image*:

> "The New Testament word for stewardship is oikonomia, from which we derive the word economy. This word means 'management of a household,' and it refers to the responsibility that is entrusted to a manager. A steward acts as an administrator of the affairs and possessions of another. Stewards are fully accountable to their masters and may act justly as did Joseph who became Potiphar's steward (Genesis 39:4-6), or unjustly as in Christ's parable of the steward who squandered his master's possessions (Luke 16:1-13). As Christians, we have been entrusted with a stewardship; the things we call our own are not really ours, but God's. We have no possessions, and we do not even own ourselves: 'Or do you not know that your body is a temple of the Holy Spirit who is in you, whom you have from God, and that you are not your own? For you have been bought with a price: therefore glorify God in your body' (1 Corinthians 6:19-20; cf. 3:23). Since we belong to Christ, we no longer have the right to self-determination."

Faithfulness has pleasing the Lord as its focus, not working for selfish gain. Note this quote by Charles Stanley:

> *"It takes a secure and humble leader to be able to serve others and help them succeed.*
>
> *"As long as we insist on writing our own stories, He cannot write His living will onto our hearts.*
>
> *"As long as we insist on forging our own paths, He cannot lead us into His paths of righteousness.*
>
> *"As long as we insist on governing our own lives, He cannot be our Sovereign King and Lord.*
>
> *"As long as we insist on living life according to our own desires, He cannot impart His desires or guide us into His wholeness, fruitfulness, and blessings.*
>
> *"As long as we feel that we are in control of our fate, we cannot experience fully the destiny he has for us. We are His workmanship. When we act otherwise, we are breaching our trust relationship with God and are refusing to submit our lives fully to Him."*

WHOLE-LIFE STEWARDSHIP

We are called to be managers of not only our the finances but of a number of other resources that the Lord has graciously given to us. This is called "whole-life stewardship." There are 7 areas where the Lord gives us resources and gifts to be used by Him in us and on His behalf: Time, Talent, Treasure, Truth, Relationships, Gospel, and Grace.

Take time, for example. Our time on earth is not controlled by us whether short or long. What we do control is how we use it, either for selfish gain or for extending God's kingdom purposes. We can learn the principles of time management to better use our time, because our time on earth is limited and once spent it can never be regained.

The Lord gives us talents and gifts, such as the innate ability to work with people or numbers. Again, we can grow and learn in these areas to order to improve; yet we are all uniquely different but wonderfully made and gifted. The Lord also fashions us with a distinct personality that is uniquely ours. The question is how are we investing our gifts? We need to realize and embrace the fact that all of life is gift and grace; we don't deserve it and cannot earn it. We are called to manage it wise and well.

Order means putting the basics in and taking the clutter out.

> *"We buy stuff we don't need with money we don't have to impress people we don't like."*
>
> – George Carlin

> *"Money never made a man happy yet, nor will it. The more a man has, the more he wants. Instead of filling a vacuum, it makes one."*
>
> –Benjamin Franklin

"But all things must be done properly and in an orderly manner" (1 Corinthians 14:40).

Order is reflected in our choices especially that lays a foundation that we can build upon or establish a godly life. Many are enslaved by fear, doubt, hatred, vices, and sin that add to life's hardship. Friend, if today you are enslaved by sin and doubt, you can be free in Christ! Only in personally knowing Christ as Lord and serving Him can you be truly free from the devil, sin and the bondage they bring (John 8:32, 36).

Order begins with reducing the clutter and gathering the right things (priorities). The next step is to put the right things in order. As we diligent pursue order, the fruit begins to take shape and comes in the form of freedom and peace. Freedom from entanglement, bondage, and busyness. As we experience freedom we then have peace in our soul. (See Ephesians 2:12; John 14:23, 16:33.)

. Freedom and peace should not be the goal of our lives. These actually can become a trap if we look to them to make us independent of problems and responsibilities and seek to entertain ourselves. We should enjoy things in this world, yet we only do so by knowing they come from God's hand. *"For you were called to freedom, brethren; only do not turn your freedom into an opportunity for the flesh, but through love serve one another"* (Galatians 5:13). Freedom and peace need to be considered as by-products of an orderly life; our focus needs to be on serving others.

PRACTICAL STEPS TO ORDER

1. Choose to obey – faithful begins (John15:2-3), clean and bearing fruit (John 14:21)
2. Become disentangled – 2 Timothy 2:4
3. Gain margin, simplify – 2 Corinthians 11:3
4. Determine "How much is enough?"

We now come to the real issue: Have we put a limit or cap on our debts, what we need, and what we desire? This is what it means to close your circle. It will take willpower and conviction to limit your lifestyle. This quote by James Dobson helps put things into perspective.

"I have concluded that the accumulation of wealth, even if I could achieve it, is an insufficient reason for living. When I reach the end of my days, a moment or two from now I must look backward on something more meaningful than the pursuit of houses, land, machines, stocks and bonds. Nor is fame any lasting benefit. I will consider my earthly existence to have been wasted unless I can recall a loving family, a consistent investment in the lives of people and an earnest attempt to serve the God who made me. Nothing else makes much sense."

Don't stop at peace and freedom; it is a "rest area," not the destination.
- Money? Think about: Debt, Spending, Saving, Giving
- Relationships? Think about: Confess, Forgive, Comfort, Care, Love
- Work? Think about: Purpose, Committed, Contribute, Excellence

SUMMARY

We must recognize that the Lord is the owner of all; He controls every circumstance and He promises to meet our every need. Our part is to be a faithful steward or manager. We are to be stewards of our whole life—Time, Talent, Treasure, Truth, Relationships, Gospel, and Grace. From stewardship we are to exercise thankfulness in all things.

The challenge we will face is that you will have push back on this from the world and even well meaning Christians. Stewardship is not easy. Society says that you earned your money and now you can spend it anyway you choose and you will be happy. The Word tells us to be faithful stewards.

The Mountain of **ORDER** requires giving up ownership and doing the right things. It is characterized by common sense. Order is where we give up control, become a steward and begin to live with discipline by giving up ownership of our self, our resources, and our will. The outcome is that we gain humility and obedience and experience freedom and peace.

- **Step 1 – Give up ownership and be a steward.** Let go of control and results. Steward the process: motive/choice/character/action
- **Step 2 – Exercise self-control and personal discipline.** Begin to form true character – integrity, humility, trustworthiness.
- **Step 3 – Do the Next, Best, Wise, Right thing.** What is in front of you, priority, use your mind and do it with excellence.
- **Step 4 – Seek to gain margin in money, work, time, relationships.** Build good habits. Clean up messes. Be at peace with others.

Seek Him first and all these things will be added to you. (See Matthew 6:30-34.) Freedom is found through being a slave. (See Romans 6:18.)

Chapter 10

THE VALLEY OF ESTABLISH

"Our Walk Is Deepened by Pruning and Abiding"
KEY DESCRIPTOR: Dependence
CHARACTERISTICS: Pruning and Abiding

The Valley of **ESTABLISH** is pivotal in the life of a Christ follower. It is at this point that we either move forward or we move back to the loop of chaos-surrender-order. God's process of "establishing" involves the following aspects: foundation, strengthen, set in place, deepen, build up, and reveal. These all involve a cost, sacrifice, and at times pain. As we walk through the Valley of **ESTABLISH**, the Lord brings us to the place of dependence upon Him; He begins to make us whole and emotionally healthy, we overcome fear, and express our gratitude back to Him.

FOUNDATION AND DEPTH

We walk and progress in life when we are on firm ground. It is hard to walk in the mud and swamps of life. This foundation is built or established by applying God's Word (Colossians 2:6-7). In practical terms, this involves living from your new identity and exercising the spiritual disciplines. Life will always send us curve balls and difficulties through no fault of our own. And it is in this pain where we are being pruned in order to bear more fruit.

Materialism and love of money have always been the greatest hindrances to a personal, living relationship with the Lord. People who are materialistic think little of sacrificing and offering anything for Him who died and gave Himself for them. After receiving Christ as Lord and Savior, we need to accept the fact that we are to live a life of service and sacrifice for Him. Only then can we be truly satisfied. You can gain the whole world but lose your own soul (Mark 8:36; 10:29-30) or, like Paul, you can lose earthly opportunities but gain Christ and lay up treasure in heaven!

The following five principles are central to "Establishing":

1. **Establishing is central to the process of going deeper with the Lord.** *"Therefore as you have received Christ Jesus the Lord, so walk in Him, having been firmly rooted and now being built up in Him and established in your faith, just as you were instructed, and overflowing with gratitude"* (Colossians 2:6-7). *"For I long to see you so that I may impart some spiritual gift to you, that you may be established"* (Romans 1:11).

2. **It creates the foundation upon which we build on lives.** *"After you have suffered for a little while, the God of all grace, who called you to His eternal glory in Christ, will Himself perfect, confirm, strengthen and establish you"* (1 Peter 5:10). *"Therefore everyone who hears these words of Mine and acts on them, may be compared to a wise man who built his house on the rock. And the rain fell, and the floods came, and the winds blew and slammed against that house; and yet it did not fall, for it had been founded on the rock. Everyone who hears these words of Mine and does not act on them, will be like a foolish man who built his house on the sand. The rain fell, and the floods came, and the winds blew and slammed against that house; and it fell—and great was its fall"* (Matthew 7:24-27). *"Therefore leaving the elementary teaching about the Christ, let us press on to maturity, not laying again a foundation of repentance from dead works and of faith toward God"* (Hebrews 6:1).

3. **It is when we are at the end of our own resources (weakness) that God's power in manifest.** *"Concerning this I implored the*

Lord three times that it might leave me. And He has said to me, 'My grace is sufficient for you, for power is perfected in weakness.' Most gladly, therefore, I will rather boast about my weaknesses, so that the power of Christ may dwell in me. Therefore I am well content with weaknesses, with insults, with distresses, with persecutions, with difficulties, for Christ's sake; for when I am weak, then I am strong" (2 Corinthians 12:8-10).

4. **It will determine the outcome of God's refinement process.** *"For we are God's fellow workers; you are God's field, God's building. According to the another is building on it. But each man must be careful how he builds on it. For no man can lay a foundation other than the one which is laid, which is Jesus Christ. Now if any man builds on the foundation with gold, silver, precious stones, wood, hay, straw, each man's work will become evident; for the day will show it because it is to be revealed with fire, and the fire itself will test the quality of each man's work. If any man's work which he has built on it remains, he will receive a reward. If any man's work is burned up, he will suffer loss; but he himself will be saved, yet so as through fire"* (1 Corinthians 3:9-15).

5. **It will clarify the true source of our strength and refuge.** *"God is our refuge and strength, A very present help in trouble....Cease striving and know that I am God; I will be exalted among the nations, I will be exalted in the earth"* (Psalms 46:1, 10). *"On God my salvation and my glory rest; the rock of my strength, my refuge is in God"* (Psalm 62:7).

WHAT DOES ESTABLISHING LOOK LIKE?

Various pictures and analogies that help us understand and practice establishing include:

- Anchor/storm – the anchor holds the ship in a fixed position in the storm
- Brick/mortar – the mortar binds the loose bricks together to build the structure
- Steel/fire – steel is tempered or annealed under temperature and pressure to vastly strengthen
- Plastic/stretch – Polypropylene when stretched is infinitely stronger
- Roots/desert – roots are deepened in the desert to find water and to hold the plant in place
- Foundation/building – the foundation must be laid for a building to stand
- Walk/feet on solid soil – to walk you must be on solid ground not quick sand
- Backbone/walking – the human body can not walk without the backbone
- Steel in concrete – concrete strength is greatly increase when there is steel wire in the core

A great example of depth determining the breadth is found in the Dubai Tower. The Dubai Tower is the largest building in the world and stands 168 stories high. The foundation is 30 stories deep. The foundation of this building is directly related to how high the building could be and must be dug and laid before the superstructure can be built. The 192 pillars and concrete platform form the foundation upon which the visible building was built. The process took many months to prepare and build this foundation before the building could begin to rise above ground level. The foundation is unseen, yet it had to be fully tested and certified to be stable before the building could begin.

These steps are similar to building the character of a leader. Character is hidden, yet must be tested to prove sure. The depth of character will ultimately determine the breadth and impact of the person. His or her character is the foundation upon which trust is built; leaders can only lead as far and fast as the trust their followers place in them.

PRUNING AND ABIDING IN THE VALLEY

As we move on from "order" to the Valley of **ESTABLISH**, there are two central themes and/or actions that make up the process of establishing dependence, and these are "pruning" and "abiding." These come directly from John 15:2-5, *"Every branch in Me that does not bear fruit, He takes away; and every branch that bears fruit, He prunes it so that it may bear more fruit. You are already clean because of the word which I have spoken to you. Abide in Me, and I in you. As the branch cannot bear fruit of itself unless it abides in the vine, so neither can you unless you abide in Me. I am the vine, you are the branches; he who abides in Me and I in him, he bears much fruit, for apart from Me you can do nothing."*

Pruning can be just as difficult and painful as the correction found in the Valley of **RECONCILE**, yet the reason is totally different. In the process of surrender in the Valley of **RECONCILE**, we may be suffering the consequences of sin or wrong behavior or at least we are being "corrected." But with "pruning" that occurs in the Valley of **ESTABLISH**, we have done nothing wrong, yet the Lord is allowing pain and struggle to grow our faith and dependence. We see that the pain is redemptive and for our good.

In the John 15 passage above we see that pruning is followed immediately by abiding in Christ. This is a process of growing deeper into the Lord. Roots must grow deeper in the desert, and the same goes for our "spiritual roots" when we experience drought conditions. While the circumstances are challenging, the outcome is good. Note the descriptions of both pruning and abiding below.

Pruning – John 15:2-3	Abiding – John 15:4-5
Difficulties, Pain	Intimacy, Identity, Indwelling
Spiritual warfare: World, Flesh, Devil	Christ as Life and Lord
God's oversight / plan	Worship
Tested by Fire	Refuge in the storm
Emotional wholeness and victory	Rest and be still to listen
Waiting on the Lord	Ministry to the Lord – Acts 13
Self-examination	Worship and Praise – Ps 73:25, Ps 95:6, Ps 96:9
Thanksgiving – Ps 100:4, 111:1	Be at home with Lord – He is our refuge
Resist the enemy; Embrace the pain	Exercise the spiritual disciplines
Decision of Dependence – Crisis of Belief	

The Valley of **ESTABLISH** requires us to make a "decision of dependence." We choose to enter in and choose to walk through this valley. If we don't, we will move backward. Faith and dependence is a choice one makes to pursue the Lord, and it is often in the face of great uncertainty from a world perspective, the possibility of pain and potential loss. *"Consider it all joy, my brethren, when you encounter various trials, knowing that the testing of your faith produces endurance. And let endurance have its perfect result, so that you may be perfect and complete, lacking in nothing"* (James 1:2-4).

WHY DOES THE LORD ALLOW THESE CHALLENGES?

The Lord desires and plans for us to increase, to be strengthened, and to grow in each of these areas:

- FAITH is Deepened
- HOPE is Clarified
- LOVE is Received

The results are for our very good.

"You too be patient; strengthen your hearts, for the coming of the Lord is near" (James 5:8).

"Strengthening the souls of the disciples, encouraging them to continue in the faith, and saying, 'Through many tribulations we must enter the kingdom of God'" (Acts 14:22).

"Your word is a lamp for my feet, a light on my path" (Psalm 119:105).

"Establish my footsteps in Your word, And do not let any iniquity have dominion over me" (Psalm 119:133).

Throughout this process we are learning to partner with the Lord by walking by faith in humility, seeking His will, pursuing intimacy with Him, thanking Him, and growing in His Word.

Paul described this process in his letter to the Philippians: *"More than that, I count all things to be loss in view of the surpassing value of knowing Christ Jesus my Lord, for whom I have suffered the loss of all things, and count them but rubbish so that I may gain Christ, that I may know Him and the power of His resurrection and the fellowship of His sufferings, being conformed to His death"* (Philippians 3:8, 10). We gain everything through losing everything.

APPLICATION

1. Be thankful in all things.
2. Lean into the challenges.
3. Acknowledge and deal with any past emotional pain and hurt in order to experience emotional healing.
4. Seek to be in community especially in times of difficulty—don't attempt going it alone.

These applications help bring about our availability and establish our lives on the solid rock of Christ and His Word. The results are that we identify with Christ and are able to stand strong in the battle.

Thank the Lord in the Difficulty

Thankfulness begins with the realization that the Lord loves us infinitely and has given us untold riches in Christ that we did not deserve. This love comes from God's immutable character, not from what we can feel or sense.

We can be thankful in all things because He is with us always. The Lord never leaves us or forsakes us. He is in control, loves you, and never gives up on you. God is always at work even when you don't recognize it. A thankful heart can change the whole way you see life! It opens up the floodgate of blessings, joy, peace, and all sorts of goodness. Developing a thankful heart can revolutionize the quality and enjoyment of one's life!

Start by saying, "Thank You, Lord!" When we express to the Lord our gratitude in any situation, we are putting tangible and practical steps to our walk with the Lord. This is both a prayer and a step of faith. Being thankful will result in being filled with joy.

> *"Devote yourselves to prayer, keeping alert in it with an attitude of thanksgiving"* (Colossians 4:2).
> *"Always giving thanks for all things in the name of our Lord Jesus Christ to God, even the Father"* (Ephesians 5:20).
> *"In everything give thanks; for this is God's will for you in Christ Jesus"* (1 Thessalonians 5:18).

Lean into Your Challenges

Problems have silver linings as they provide you opportunities to grow. The question is how do we perceive the challenges or difficulties in front of us. Do we embrace the challenges or fight against them? Obstacles turn into opportunities when we see them from God's perspective.

Dealing with Hurt

Often times in the pruning process we will be hurt and taken advantage of by others. This will happen—I guarantee it. The question becomes how to deal with it. We first must acknowledge the hurt and know that we are not alone in the process. We must forgive and release the other party.

Then we are called to love and pray for our adversaries (see Matthew 5:44). and *"to do good to those who hate you"* (Luke 6:27). In these times of hurt we must keep our emotions in check in order to keep the devil at bay. This opens doors for the Lord to work, and the burden is on his shoulders, not ours.

Living in Community

The one thing we must watch out for is becoming isolated. This is exactly where the enemy wants us to be. If we are alone in our challenges and pain, the problems magnify and our emotions give us false signals. We need one another, God does not call us or expect us to go through the pain by ourselves.

> *"Beneath all our problems there are desperately hurting souls that must find the nourishment only community can provide or die. The greatest need in modern civilization is the development of communities—true communities where the heart of God is home, where the humble and wise learn to shepherd those on the path behind them, where trusting strugglers lock arms with others as together they journey on."*
>
> – Larry Crabb

SUMMARY: VICTORY IN THIS VALLEY

As we walk through the Valley of **ESTABLISH** there are incredible results. Not only do we grow in our faith and in intimacy with the Lord here are five additional outcomes.

1. We bear much Fruit – John 15:5
2. We flourish – Psalm 93:12-15
3. We honor and glorify the Lord
4. We obtain security, satisfaction, and significance.
5. We gain approval from the Lord – Hebrews 11:39-40

Establish depth in your walk through pruning and abiding.

- **Step 1 – Embrace the pruning, hurt, and pain.** Learn the lessons for growth. You will be tested. Ask 'What'? not 'Why?'
- **Step 2 – Be intentional, grow in the Word.** Renew your mind. Pursue Intimacy through the spiritual disciplines.
- **Step 3 – Be thankful and grateful in all things.** See the good in the bad. There are opportunities. Be Positive.
- **Step 4 – Grow in your Identity. Heal emotional pain.** Receive security, significance and satisfaction. Grow in dependence.

When you are weak, you are strong. (See 2 Corinthians 12:10.)
Grow more fruit by being pruned. (See John 15:2-3.)

Chapter 11

THE MOUNTAIN OF MATURITY

"Seek God's Will Only – Exercise His Wisdom Fully"
KEY DESCRIPTOR: Wisdom
CHARACTERISTICS: Contentment and Generosity

THE JOURNEY CONTINUES -
CLIMBING THE MOUNTAIN OF MATURITY

The Mountain of **MATURITY** is distinguished by spiritual growth. Having godly values, wisdom, contentment, and generosity can only take place as we realize we don't have the power and strength to battle the world and the enemy but the Lord does. He is the source of ultimate victory. Maturity is not a goal but it's the outcome of a process that equips us to be fully engaged in God's purposes. We seek His will not our will.

God allowed Paul a "thorn in his flesh" which kept him humble and ever dependent on God. Three times he prayed for the thorn's removal, but God said that His grace is ever sufficient. In this Paul rejoiced! Would you like the world to see the power of Christ rest in you? Then serve God faithfully in spite of sickness, trials, and troubles. Rejoice in God! We all have weaknesses that God can use to make us aware of our limitations and keep us humble and useful!

"Maturity is: The ability to stick with a job until it's finished; The ability to do a job without being supervised; The ability to carry money without spending it; and The ability to bear an injustice without wanting to get even."
— Abigail Van Buren

"Maturity is the ability to think, speak and act your feelings within the bounds of dignity. The measure of your maturity is how spiritual you become during the midst of your frustrations."
— Samuel Ullman

What is Maturity? Maturity is being fully developed, possessing experience, and exercising wisdom. It is beyond such typical markers as age, knowledge, or wealth. Vines dictionary defines maturity as being perfect or complete. Biblically speaking, it involves a choice to seek and follow the Lord's will only, not asking the Lord to bless one's own plans. Maturity models wisdom and good judgment—it's applied knowledge. Being mature is doing what you know to be right and true. It is often described as "Obedience in the long direction." Maturity is being made whole, especially in emotions and pain. It also takes full responsibility and doesn't point blame first. In becoming mature, there is a part we play and a part the Lord plays.

"When I was a child, I talked like a child, I thought like a child, I reasoned like a child. When I became a man, I put childish ways behind me. Now we see but a poor reflection as in a mirror; then we shall see face to face. Now I know in part; then I shall know fully, even as I am fully known" (1 Corinthians 13:11-12 NIV).

"I press on toward the goal to win the prize for which God has called me heavenward in Christ Jesus. All of us who are mature should take such a view of things. And if on some point

you think differently, that too God will make clear to you. Only let us live up to what we have already attained" (Philippians 3:14-16 NIV).

DIGGING DEEPER

Maturity is a hallmark of being a spiritual Christian, and Scripture implores us to grow up and become mature. Jesus alludes to this in the parable of the sower, the soils, and the seed while Paul specifically lays out maturity as the goal of the church and ministry:

"And He gave some as apostles, and some as prophets, and some as evangelists, and some as pastors and teachers, for the equipping of the saints for the work of service, to the building up of the body of Christ; until we all attain to the unity of the faith, and of the knowledge of the Son of God, to a mature man, to the measure of the stature which belongs to the fullness of Christ. As a result, we are no longer to be children, tossed here and there by waves and carried about by every wind of doctrine, by the trickery of men, by craftiness in deceitful scheming; but speaking the truth in love, we are to grow up in all aspects into Him who is the head, even Christ, from whom the whole body, being fitted and held together by what every joint supplies, according to the proper working of each individual part, causes the growth of the body for the building up of itself in love" (Ephesians 4:11-15).

John writes a similar theme of maturity in 1 John 2:12-14 (NIV).

"I am writing to you, dear children, because your sins have been forgiven on account of his name.

"I am writing to you, fathers, because you have known him who is from the beginning.

"I am writing to you, young men, because you have overcome the evil one.

"I write to you, dear children, because you have known the Father.

"I write to you, fathers, because you have known him who is from the beginning.

"I write to you, young men, because you are strong, the word of God lives in you, and you have overcome the evil one."

PATH TO MATURITY
Demonstrated by choices; directed by hope; displayed by faith and love

Fundamentally maturity comes down to the choices we make—do we trust the Lord to do His part, and do we take responsibility for our part? When one is mature, there is a quality of inner peace and wholeness, a sense of deep security, satisfaction, and significance. We accept who and where we are, yet we continually seek growth. Love and grace have been fully received and are being given out to others. We are a conduit of God working in and through us. Maturity exercises the spiritual disciplines as a way of life, bears much fruit in all of its relationships, and exhibits the fullness of Christ.

PATH TO MATURITY Demonstrated by Choices; directed by hope; displayed by faith & love			
	Little Children	Adult	Servant Leader
Marks of:	Disorder/Chaos Fun and pleasure Innocent, Naive Little discipline Inconsistency Much activity Black and white view	Order Listens and walks with God Responsitiblity Developed in speaking, thinking and reasoning Fruit	Maturity and Wisdom Outward focus Kingdom oriented Handling ambiguity Humility and sacrifical Developed intentionality in purpose, eternal things and investing in others Much/Multiplying fruit
Spiritual Issues	Limited spiritual understanding and inconsistency in disciplines Focus on today and temporal Knowledge growth	Possesses a disciplined spiritual life of the word and prayer Focus on the temporal future Model integrity (thoughts and actions the same)	Spiritual life is marked by intimacy and a deep desire to glorify God and see His Kingdom prevail Focus on the eternal while living in the temporal Wisdom – applying knowledge Intentional investment in others
Leadership Arenas	Lead self - money, lifestyle, choices Need structure and some level of control	Lead wife, family, a disciple Need priorities and practice	Lead a team or many Need to be creative and heart focused
Issues of Leadership to Consider	Emotions – easily angered / reactionary Demanding, Get rid of threats Self-focused and self-centered Driven to Results and outcome, Bigger, better, faster Taking Actions based on desires	Know their emotions but don't live by them Able to delegate Able to work with others on an equal basis Results and Process are both important Stewardship Able to Reflect	Use emotions to grow self and inspire others w/o affecting actions Empowered leader, Oversight of others Develop others Legacy and heritage are important, not immediate results. Giving and investing
Growth Issues	Take responsibility Leave home Behavior	Be Faithful / Trustworthy Establish a home Values	Impart your life Help others leave and establish a home Spiritual
Growth Application	Spiritual, time, finances, work and relationships, emotions	Wife and Family Ministry involvement	Kingdom Teams

Mature individuals know themselves—their strengths and weaknesses. Only then can they take hold of the power of Christ, knowing that when they are weak, they are strong (see 2 Corinthians 12:10).

Moving from Child to an Adult (developed in speaking, thought and reasoning)

Childish people are consumed with worries, riches, and continual pleasure seeking: *"The seed which fell among the thorns, these are the ones who have heard, and as they go on their way they are choked with worries and riches and pleasures of this life, and bring no fruit to maturity"* (Luke 8:14).

"Even a child makes himself known by his acts, by whether his conduct is pure and upright" (Proverbs 20:11 ESV).

"Brothers and sisters, stop thinking like children. In regard to evil be infants, but in your thinking be adults" (1 Corinthians 14:20 NIV).

"In fact, though by this time you ought to be teachers, you need someone to teach you the elementary truths of God's word all over again. You need milk, not solid food! Anyone who lives on milk, being still an infant, is not acquainted with the teaching about righteousness. But solid food is for the mature, who by constant use have trained themselves to distinguish good from evil" (Hebrews 5:12-14 NIV).

We will look at six areas where a child needs to mature, and we'll consider our personal walk first. Then we will look at how to move from being a "childish" leader to an "adult" leader. Let's begin by looking at what it takes to for a child to become an adult. What would you say it takes to make this transition? This verse indicates that the process begins in our heart and in our thinking: *"Brethren, do not be children in your thinking; yet in evil be infants, but in your thinking be **mature**"* (1 Corinthians 14:20).

1. **Spiritual:** Are we taking responsibility for our sins and sinful attitudes? In this area, one needs to recognize that sin is sin, and although we are forgiven, we need to recognize our flesh patterns and address them. Order is seeking to be pure before one can grow into intimacy. It is exercising discipline to grow in the word and prayer. Begin to have a desire for intimacy.

2. **Time:** How does we utilize our time? Are we undisciplined in managing our time (sleep late, stay up late, fritter away time, put things off to the last minute, try to do multiple tasks at once and get nothing done)? Order is being able to balance the demands and responsibilities that we have accepted.

3. **Finances:** Are we able to provide for themselves? A child needs to leave home and not rely on the parents resources for daily living. Do we manage our finances well or do we spend all we have, or worse yet, live off of credit cards? Do we display a love of money or is it a means to an end? Order is living within our means. We begin to live on less than we make and start to save.

4. **Work:** Are we working? 2 Thessalonians 3:10 says, *"If anyone is not willing to work, then he is not to eat either."* One needs to work; it is not optional. A next step is to grow in realizing the value of hard work and doing things with excellence. Work needs to precede the fun, pleasure, or entertainment. It is easy for these to be the end; they are not. Work is a means of how the Lord will provide for us. It is critical to understand that the Lord is the ultimate provider and work is also an arena to display God working though us, otherwise we can fall into the trap of work being the ultimate end. Order is working and beginning to enjoy what we do.

5. **Relationships:** Do we have good relationships and seek to put others ahead of ourselves? Relationships involve grow by investing time, care and resources; they don't come by taking. In the words of Christ, "it is better to give than receive." Order is having healthy relationships and friends to enjoy life with.

6. **Emotions:** Do we manage our emotions and feelings, or are we driven by them? For instance, how do we handle disappointment? Do we struggle with anger? Order is being aware of emotions, not stuffing them, and able to forgive and work through hurts.

The process of a child becoming an adult is not instantaneous; it can be slow and painful. We also can be an adult in some areas and not in others. The Lord will have to grow us in these areas. The goal for a child is to put away "childish" speaking, thinking, and reasoning and grow into the useful leader the Lord wants them to be. An adult leader is then able to lead a spouse, provide for their home and enter into having a fruitful ministry.

Moving from Adult to Servant Leader (intentionality in purpose, eternal things and investing in others)

As we stated, an adult has moved from chaos to order; they begin to provide for themselves and those who they are directly responsible for. To move from adult to servant leader is also a slow and sometimes difficult process. Few truly arrive at full maturity, yet this is God's intention and desire for us. In fact, He gives us all of the resources to move to this level because we have Christ! *"But speaking the truth in love, we are to grow up in all aspects into Him who is the head, even Christ"* (Ephesians 4:15). Why do so few ever arrive?

What does "Maturity" look like for you personally in each of these arenas (Spiritual, Time, Finances, Work, Relationships, Emotions)? What will it take for you to become mature in those areas where you are still a child?

Examine the following verses and consider the process of moving from adult to servant leader.

> *"TTherefore let us leave the elementary doctrine of Christ and go on to maturity, not laying again a foundation of repentance from dead works and of faith toward God"* (Hebrews 6:1 ESV).

"All Scripture is God-breathed and is useful for teaching, rebuking, correcting and training in righteousness, so that the man of God may be thoroughly equipped for every good work" (2 Timothy 3:16-17 NIV).

CONTENTMENT AND GENEROSITY

Finally, maturity results in two primary actions and attitudes—Contentment and Generosity:

"Not that I speak from want, for I have learned to be content in whatever circumstances I am. I know how to get along with humble means, and I also know how to live in prosperity; in any and every circumstance I have learned the secret of being filled and going hungry, both of having abundance and suffering need. I can do all things through Him who strengthens me" (Philippians 4:11-13).

"Now this I say, he who sows sparingly will also reap sparingly, and he who sows bountifully will also reap bountifully. Each one must do just as he has purposed in his heart, not grudgingly or under compulsion, for God loves a cheerful giver. And God is able to make all grace abound to you, so that always having all sufficiency in everything, you may have an abundance for every good deed" (2 Corinthians 9:6-8).

Contentment

"Contentment is the only real wealth."
— Alfred Nobel (founder of Nobel Prize)

"He is not fool to lose what he can not keep to gain what he can not lose."
— Jim Elliot

As we can attain order in our finances, we first find freedom and then peace, but these do not necessarily bring happiness and joy. Happiness and joy are only by-products of being content no matter how much wealth and resources we have. Contentment doesn't mean you are happy in the bad times. It means you are satisfied with life because you know that God has things under control.

Note the definition of contentment: Contentment is a mental or emotional state of satisfaction drawn from being at ease in one's situation, body and mind. Contentment is a state of having accepted one's situation and results in happiness.

Jesus tells the following story with a simple message, our lives are not to be filled with the riches of this world and all of its greed for possessions and power. Our lives are to be rich toward God. In addition, we will have to give an account of our actions. We will answer to the Lord for what we have done with what we have been given. Contentment is the critical step in living this out.

> *"He said to them, 'Beware, and be on your guard against every form of greed; for not even when one has an abundance does his life consist of his possessions.' And He told them a parable, saying, 'The land of a rich man was very productive. And he began reasoning to himself, saying, "What shall I do, since I have no place to store my crops?" Then he said, "This is what I will do: I will tear down my barns and build larger ones, and there I will store all my grain and my goods. And I will say to my soul, 'Soul, you have many goods laid up for many years to come; take your ease, eat, drink and be merry.'" But God said to him, 'You fool! This very night your soul is required of you; and now who will own what you have prepared?' So is the man who stores up treasure for himself, and is not rich toward God"* (Luke 12:15-21).

Principles on Contentment

We will examine seven principles on contentment and how to be content. First note three Scripture passages that reference being content:

"Make sure that your character is free from the love of money, being content with what you have; for He Himself has said, "I will never desert you, nor will I ever forsake you" (Hebrews 13:5).

"He who loves money will not be satisfied with money, nor he who loves wealth with his income; this also is vanity" (Ecclesiastes 5:10 ESV).

"Give me neither poverty nor riches; feed me with the food that is needful for me, lest I be full and deny you and say, "Who is the Lord?" or lest I be poor and steal and profane the name of my God" (Proverbs 30:8-9 ESV).

1. **Contentment at its core is an issue of CONTROL and RESULTS.**

    We previously looked at 1 Chronicles 29:11-12 from which we understand that God owns it all. We also concluded that the Lord is in control and the overseer of the results in this world. If we embrace this fact, we can rest in the character and grace of the Lord. Resting in the Lord is tantamount to being content. Psalm 23:1 says, *"The Lord is my shepherd, I shall not want."* David wrote this Psalm. You can hear the contentment in his voice because he knows that he will never be left wanting. God is the shepherd and we are the sheep. God will take care of His sheep, and we need to trust in His promises. *"Come to Me all who are weary and heavy-laden, and I will give you rest"* (Matthew 11:28).

    We also find a great promise in Philippians 4:19, *"And my God will supply every need of yours according to his riches in glory in Christ Jesus"* (ESV).

Contentment helps us answer these questions:

- How much is enough?
- Who controls the flow of all things into my life?
- Does God have my best interests at heart?
- How do I respond to suffering and difficulties?

Ken Boa speaks to the issue of contentment. "It is only when we allow Christ to determine the content of our lives that we can discover the secret of contentment. Instead of comparing ourselves with others, we must realize that the Lord alone knows what is best for us and loves us enough to use our present circumstances to accomplish eternal good. We can be content when we put our hope in His character rather than our own concept of how our lives should appear."

2. **Contentment requires an eternal rather than a temporal perspective of life.**

This temporal life will determine my eternity and its condition. My reward is found in only heaven. We need to take hold of this idea found in Matthew 6:21, *"For where your treasure is, there your heart will be also."* Our hearts are only satisfied with the things of the eternal.

3. **The secret about contentment is that it can be learned.**

"Not that I am speaking of being in need, for I have learned in whatever situation I am to be content. I know how to be brought low, and I know how to abound. In any and every circumstance, I have learned the secret of facing plenty and hunger, abundance and need. I can do all things through Him who strengthens me" (Philippians 4:11-13 ESV).

Paul really drives home the main point of contentment in these three verses. "I am to be content" means that there is a predetermined attitude for all situations. It is planned and through self-discipline it can be achieved. "I can do all things through

Him who strengthens me" must be engraved in our hearts and minds. When we focus on the Word, we can respond appropriately in all circumstances. Christ is our Savior and Lord. He won't let us down. He will strengthen us to be content.

4. **Life is not found in our possessions but in Christ alone. He is our life.**

"And he said to them, 'Take care, and be on your guard against all covetousness, for one's life does not consist in the abundance of his possessions'" (Luke 12:15 ESV).

Coveting is the opposite of contentment. If jealousy of others pushes you to getting things that they have then you are missing the point. Jesus said, "Life does not consist in the abundance of...possessions." Don't be swayed by the glamour and prestige around you. It is all an attempt by Satan to keep you worldly minded and not eternally minded.

"For the sake of Christ, then, I am content with weaknesses, insults, hardships, persecutions, and calamities. For when I am weak, then I am strong" (2 Corinthians 12:10 ESV).

There is an important point here: "for the sake of Christ." This is the reason why we all can be content. Christ left perfection in heaven to come down to the most disorderly place ever. He came down willingly, knowing that men would lead Him to a horrific death on a cross, so that we could be saved and be holy before God. That is why we can be content in all of the bad stuff. If Christ loved us enough to die for us all, then being content is nothing compared to the gift we have been given. We can be thankful in all things because Christ loved us all of the way to the cross.

"Keep your life free from love of money, and be content with what you have, for he has said, 'I will never leave you nor forsake you'" (Hebrews 13:5 ESV).

If your full trust is in the Lord then you can be assured that His promises are true. God will never leave nor forsake you.

Therefore, there is no need to fret. God has planned out every day of your life, so ask Him for guidance and allow Him to lead you.

Contentment begins with and in our relationship with Jesus Christ. "The thief comes only to steal and kill and destroy; I came that they may have life, and have it abundantly" (John 10:10).

Note the idea we have been given magnificent promises in 2 Peter 1:2-4, *"Grace and peace be multiplied to you in the knowledge of God and of Jesus our Lord; seeing that His divine power has granted to us everything pertaining to life and godliness, through the true knowledge of Him who called us by His own glory and excellence. For by these He has granted to us His precious and magnificent promises, so that by them you may become partakers of the divine nature."*

Finally we in obedience and possess an overflowing gratitude. *"Therefore as you have received Christ Jesus the Lord, so walk in Him, having been firmly rooted and now being built up in Him and established in your faith, just as you were instructed, and overflowing with gratitude"* (Colossians 2:6-7).

5. **Godliness with contentment is a means of great gain.**

    "But godliness with contentment is great gain, for we brought nothing into the world, and we cannot take anything out of the world. But if we have food and clothing, with these we will be content" (1 Timothy 6:6-8 ESV).

    We experience great gain in our heart, now and in eternity, when we exercise contentment with godliness. The world is out for gain: cars, houses, fame, etc. These verses are conveying that we need to be satisfied with what we have. Not that cars, houses and fame are bad, but if we are pushing for these kinds of things then there may be a heart issue with contentment that needs to be looked at. And as Paul said, "we cannot take anything out of the world." Why strive so hard for material things that mean nothing in the end?

6. **The pursuit of contentment is a spiritual battle.**

Pursuing contentment is a spiritual battle in which we will have opposition from the world and the devil. It will not be easy. We also will have to die to our flesh and meeting its desires and wants. We must be careful not to be too busy, as this will rob us of joy and contentment. We live in the constant pressure and temptation of the enemy to pursue gain things and being defined by things and people. There is no let up.

7. **Contentment is more than freedom.**

Order frees us from worry so we may exercise maturity to serve and bless others. Contentment is not just For us, it is a state where we can help others. *"For you were called to freedom, brethren; only do not turn your freedom into an opportunity for the flesh, but through love serve one another"* (Galatians 5:13).

"Therefore I tell you, do not be anxious about your life, what you will eat or what you will drink, nor about your body, what you will put on. Is not life more than food, and the body more than clothing? Look at the birds of the air: they neither sow nor reap nor gather into barns, and yet your Heavenly Father feeds them. Are you not of more value than they?" (Matthew 6:25-26 ESV).

Worry is also the complete opposite of contentment. God loves us. He will take care of us. When you worry about things, you are not putting your full trust in God.

When we are in a frenzied pursuit for material things we will never find contentment. Many Christians get sucked into the swamp of discontent. Are you a contented Christian? Think over this past week: Was your time spent pursuing godliness with contentment, or was it consumed with going after material things? I'm not talking about the basics—food, clothing, and shelter. I'm talking about a lifestyle marked by the pursuit of all of the junk that Madison Avenue tries to convince us that we need.

Four Barriers to Pursuing Contentment

Contentment is not easy to achieve and hard to maintain. There are four things that will block us or will eat away at contentment like a cancer. These simply are:

1. Competing,
2. Comparing,
3. Counting,
4. Controlling.

Competition is when we use other people to lift us or that we try to get our identify needs meet by winning and or outdoing someone else. We are implored to compete to win the prize, yet that is competing with ourselves to do our best. Comparing is the devil's game to tell us that we need more, or we are not as good as someone else because they have more. Counting is good in that we need accurate numbers and understanding where we are financially, yet when we count to prove our self worth or as a scorecard of self made progress, the results will be disaster. Controlling people or a situation is only an opportunity for the flesh to rise up and be in charge. Watch out for these 4 C's!

THE POWER OF GENEROSITY

As we live in contentment we can learn the power of generosity. Generosity is an attribute with many great qualities: being generous has a power associated with it, generosity is attractive to others, it grows and extends to people's lives, and it expands God's Kingdom. We see this in Jesus' parable of "The Good Samaritan" (see Luke 10:30-37). In the story we see generosity lived out even when the consequences could have been hurtful or devastating. The story shows us that we can be merciful and generous to anyone if we allow the Lord to direct us. It is a picture of God and His grace toward us.

> *"Generosity is what keeps the things we own from owning us."*
> – Eugene Cho
>
> *"Do all the good you can, by all the means you can, in all the ways you can, in all the places you can, at all the times you can, to all the people you can, as long as ever you can."*
> – John Wesley

We are Blessed to be a Blessing

We have been blessed with many spiritual gifts and treasures, but they are not for ourselves. We are to be conduits (branches) for God to work through to bear much fruit, which includes the fruit of the spirit: love, joy, peace, patience, kindness, goodness, faith, meekness and self-control. We have been given (blessed with) these fruits in order to reflect the love of the Lord, to grow, and minister to others. We are called to do this generously.

Generosity Begins with the Lord and Reflects His Heart

God is very generous with us: unlimited and forever forgiveness (past, present, and future), unconditional love, the riches of an eternal life, and the fruit of Spirit. His gifts are infinite, unmeasureable, and undeserved. The impact of His grace and gifts should overwhelm us and create a thirst or desire to take hold of what we possess.

> *"For this reason I bow my knees before the Father, from whom every family in heaven and on earth derives its name, that He would grant you, according to the riches of His glory, to be strengthened with power through His Spirit in the inner man, so that Christ may dwell in your hearts through faith; and that you, being rooted and grounded in love, may be able to comprehend with all the saints what is the breadth and length and height and depth, and to know the love of Christ which surpasses knowledge, that you may be filled up to all the full-*

ness of God. Now to Him who is able to do far more abundantly beyond all that we ask or think, according to the power that works within us, to Him be the glory in the church and in Christ Jesus to all generations forever and ever. Amen.” (Ephesians 3:14-21).

We are Already Wealthy

Our riches in Christ make us wealthy beyond belief. We have been given unfathomable riches of being “in Christ.” The following are truths that help us understand and motivate us to be generous. The following statements are in the “first person” so you can personally identify with them.

- My worth and significance are found solely in Christ (which is forever and unchanging) and not in performance or in a position.
- Because of my worth in Christ, I am free from the opinions of others while learning from them.
- In this freedom from opinions, I can truly serve and love others (value and honor people).
- Because of this freedom, I can give away power or empower others.
- Because of my security in Christ, I can be process focused vs. results oriented or bottom line driven.
- “In Christ” I am free from the bondage to sin among which pride is one of the chief ones.
- His love and acceptance give me a security that helps me examine my motives and purify my motives.
- When my needs are met, I can give my life away and not try and manipulate situations or other people in order to meet those needs.

We have been brought with a price. *“You are not your own, for you were bought with a price. So glorify God in your body”* (1 Corinthians 6:19-20 ESV). You are of infinite worth in God's eyes.

David Wilkerson teaches on how much we have in Christ:

> *"Christ is the treasure chest in the field. And in Him, I've found all that I'll ever need. No more trying to find purpose in ministry. No more looking for fulfillment in family or friends. No more needing to build something for God, or to be a success, or to feel useful. No more keeping up with the crowd, or trying to prove something. No more searching for ways to please people. No more trying to think or reason my way out of difficulties.*
>
> *"I've found what I'm looking for. My treasure, my pearl, is Christ. And all that the Owner asks of me is, 'David, I love you. Let me adopt you. I've already signed the papers with my own Son's blood. You're now a joint heir with him of everything I possess.'*
>
> *"What a bargain. I give up my filthy rags of self-reliance and good works. I lay aside my worn-out shoes of striving. I leave behind my sleepless nights on the streets of doubt and fear. And in return, I am adopted by a King. This is what happens when you seek the pearl, the treasure, till you find him. Jesus offers you everything he is. He brings you joy, peace, purpose, holiness. And He becomes your everything—your waking, your sleeping, your morning, afternoon, and evening."*

We have been an infinite storehouse of eternal treasure, yet we must receive the gift, unwrap it, and put it into practice. Otherwise it is like having all of the gifts under the Christmas tree and we leave them there unwrapped. We have been given so much that we often take grace for granted. We must never be complacent with the gifts and resources given to us.

Our Role in Being Generous

We have been blessed in order to be a blessing. Exercising generosity our whole life—all of our resources, from God's incredible gifts to our time and talent and finances. Examine the following verses and reflect on our role in generosity.

> *"And if I give all my possessions to feed the poor, and if I surrender my body to be burned, but do not have love, it profits me nothing"* (1 Corinthians 13:3).
>
> *"Remember the words of the Lord Jesus, that He Himself said, 'It is more blessed to give than to receive'"* (Acts 20:35).
>
> *"Now this I say, he who sows sparingly will also reap sparingly, and he who sows bountifully will also reap bountifully. Each one must do just as he has purposed in his heart, not grudgingly or under compulsion, for God loves a cheerful giver. And God is able to make all grace abound to you, so that always having all sufficiency in everything, you may have an abundance for every good deed"* (2 Corinthians 9:6-8).
>
> *"There is one who scatters, and yet increases all the more, and there is one who withholds what is justly due, and yet it results only in want. The generous man will be prosperous, and he who waters will himself be watered"* (Proverbs 11:24-25).

Exercising Generosity

For us to practice the power of generosity consider the following six elements:

Foundation

1. **Preparation:** We begin with 1 Timothy 6:17-18 as it tells us to fix our hope on the certainty of God. We need to be practicing stewardship and surrender, we need to make wise lifestyle choices with our finances to be in a position to give and do it generously. The final part of preparation is to be content with what we have been given.

God's Part

2. **Possession:** We receive God's infinite love, gifts, and riches through Christ and we possess it. We make it ours to enjoy and live from (Galatians 2:20).

3. **Promise:** The Lord makes us a promise in 2 Corinthians 9:6-7 that if we are generous we will reap generously. God loves a cheerful giver.

Our Part

4. **Practice:** We need to be thankful in all things. We are asked to give and give freely.

5. **Product:** Generous people are attractive. We glorify the Lord and people love to connect with us. We are a light to the world. Generous people are filled with love to give away.

6. **Purpose:** Generosity has a purpose, which is to glorify the Lord, to extend God's Kingdom purposes, and make a difference in this world.

> "Contrary to our culture, the biblical doctrine of grace humbles us without degrading us, and elevates us without inflating us. It tells us that apart from Christ, we have nothing and can do nothing of eternal value. We are spiritually impotent and inadequate without Him, and we must not put our confidence in the flesh (Philippians 3:3). On the other hand, grace also tells us that we have become new creatures in Christ, having been transferred from the kingdom of darkness to the kingdom of His light, life, and love. In Him, we now enjoy complete forgiveness from sins and limitless privileges as unconditionally accepted members of God's family. Our past has been changed because of our new heredity in Christ, and our future is secure because of our new destiny as members of His body."
>
> – Ken Boa, *Conformed to His Image*

Observations about generosity and people:

- Generous people have a much better outlook on their life and their circumstances.
- Generous people work from an attitude of abundance rather than scarcity or limitations.
- Generosity is attractive and attracts people.
- You don't need anything more in order to practice generosity.
- It is much more than giving; it is loving with no strings attached.
- It is much more than money; it is our life invested in people.
- Generosity is usually the result of our maturity in the Lord.
- We can walk with the Lord, give and tithe, and have good relationships and yet, not practice generosity.
- Generosity will have eternal consequences that cannot be measured in our lifetimes.
- The lack of generosity leads to holding on to things and eventually those things owning us.
- Ungenerous people end up becoming isolated and relationships are more like acquaintances.
- The ungenerous person tends not to trust others believing they want something from them.

APPLICATION

In the process of becoming mature, we are called to practice contentment and generosity. As we make application, there are two concrete steps we can take: practicing simplicity and developing a clear purpose for our life.

Practicing Simplicity

A key practice in becoming and living in contentment is to live a life of simplicity. We live in complex times with technology and the speed with which we get around, and it can be overwhelming. To be content is live free from the things of this world that entangle us, illustrated by the soldier described in 2 Timothy 2:4.

There is an insight about living in simplicity in 2 Corinthians 11:3, *"But I am afraid that, as the serpent deceived Eve by his craftiness, your minds will be led astray from the simplicity and purity of devotion to Christ."* Complexity and having more is a deception of the enemy. We think we own and have things that make life better, but in reality the things own us because we have to manage them and look after them. Life with complexity maybe quicker, but it is not better.

How can you simplify your life? Give old stuff away and downsize. You will be amazed when the "space" of your life is free from stuff and then filled with the Lord and people.

Maturity is Marked by a Clear Purpose of Life

"The mass of men lead lives of quiet desperation."
— Henry David Thoreau

The need of the hour is for people to possess a passion and purpose for life. Many people who do not have a written life purpose statement lack clarity of focus and will not be as fruitful as they could be. A lack of purpose leads to many disastrous ends with numerous bad consequences. Here are just a few:

1. You are frustrated because you are not making progress and cannot seem to get ahead.
2. Busyness wins because there are no clear priorities.
3. Discontentment and discouragement occurs because you are comparing and looking around to see if others are getting ahead.
4. You have little or no lasting fruit to show for the mountains of activity being produced. There is no correlation between the work and the results.
5. Without clarity of focus, we end up pursuing the toys and trinkets of this world (wrong hope), we follow people and organizations who let us down (misplaced hope), or we live in utter despair (no hope).

The Lord had you in mind before the beginning of the world, and He had a plan of how you would fit into His greater plan. In realizing this, we conclude that the first question is not "What is God's purpose for *my life*?" but rather it is "What is God's purpose?" His ultimate purpose is to rule and reign in this world and beyond. We are made in His image (spiritual), designed to glorify Him in our lives for eternity.

Where do we begin? Let me suggest two questions to ask that will start the ball rolling. Go out to the end of your life and, looking back, ask the first question—*"What do I want my life to add up to?"* Our lives need to add up to more than money, power, position, etc.

For the second question, go out 200 years and look back and ask, *"What do I want to leave behind?"* This will center your focus on legacy and what is eternal. A 200-year view will help you look beyond cultural trends and issues to focus on what will last.

Finding purpose is a spiritual issue and it must begin with the Lord. Three principles about purpose must be laid as the foundation for a purpose to be strong and lasting.

First Question Principle

As we have noted previously, "What is God's purpose for my life?" is not the first or right question! It is not about us. The first question is "What is God's purpose?" We must begin with God and His perspective. From this answer, we rightly ask, "How do I fit into His plan?" When we submit our lives, plans, desires to the Lord, He will shape us to meet His plan. This is a subtle yet radical difference! We must fit into His perfect game plan; otherwise we are attempting to have God bless our faulty agenda and desires.

FOR to FROM Principle

God is not interested or impressed in what you are going to do for Him. He doesn't need you nor will you affect His final outcome. On one hand this may seem harsh or it may seem like word games (semantics). Neither is the case.

If the focus of our life and activities is on doing or being something for the Lord, we place ourselves as necessary or crucial to God's plans. We are not. Although God loves each and every one of us unconditionally and He paid the ultimate sacrifice for us, His Son's death on the cross, His goal and plan, are central. We enter into this plan from God, and we participate as He directs. We don't contribute to God's work. So my purpose individually or in any organization should not begin with "doing this or that for Christ."

Power of Purpose Principle

A God-given purpose holds, directs, and motivates our lives. It brings alignment, simplicity, and focus to all aspects of life. In addition it activates the synergistic power of God to work through us to accomplish far more than we could dream or imagine. We cannot generate this power on our own, it comes from God alone.

A life purpose is a simple statement of what the Lord wants from and with your life. How we connect with Him and how we connect with others in this life we have been given on this earth is the reason you exist, the cause behind your living now on this planet.

- Who am I serving? (This can begin with spouse or family, yet it should extend beyond them.)
- What value or influence do I bring to the table?
- What changes have I seen in others whom I have served?
- What do these people need? (Knowing these needs helps us understand what and how to serve.)
- What have I been given and what do I possess?
- What gifts, talents, skills, and life experiences do I have?
- How can I engage these resources?

Be patient: This may take several times of rewriting over a period of time to refine and polish. Discuss this with some close, personal friends. Talk to someone who has done this. Ask them to share their personal statement with you and share how they arrived at it. Sign your name at the bottom of your statement.

SUMMARY

Maturity seeks God's will only, exercising His wisdom fully: Grow Up, Gain Wisdom, Give it Away.

- **Step 1 – See a bigger picture of life and circumstances.** It is not about you. It is about God's will alone.
- **Step 2 – Always make application of the Word, it is better than knowledge.** The Word creates wisdom which comes from Him.
- **Step 3 – Work towards balance, stability, and calmness in all things.** Be the hope and peace for others.
- **Step 4 – Give generously in all areas of your life (time, talent, treasure, truth, relationships).** It will come back to bless you.

Do not seek my will, but thy will. (See Matthew 26:39; John 5:30, 6:38.)
We gain everything by counting it all as loss. (See Philippians 3:7-10.)

Chapter 12

THE VALLEY OF SACRIFICE

"Put Others Ahead of Self through Serving"
KEY DESCRIPTOR: Others
CHARACTERISTICS: Serving and Investing

SACRIFICE IS FOCUSED ON OTHERS AND SERVES THEM.

Sacrifice that leads to serving is the only path to true fulfillment. If we only focus on ourselves, what we are doing, how mature and generous we are, we will stop growing and not fulfill God's best. Maturity always leads to focusing on others. As we embark on this journey through the Valley of **SACRIFICE**, we will examine its three key components: being a servant leader, engaging in ministry, and involvement in community. Note Paul's service in Philippians 2:17, *"But even if I am being poured out as a drink offering upon the sacrifice and service of your faith, I rejoice and share my joy with you all."*

Let's begin by understanding what a sacrificial mindset looks like.

"And I will very gladly <u>spend</u> and <u>be spent</u> for you; though the more abundantly I love you, <u>the less I be loved</u>" (2 Corinthians 12:15 KJV).

We can all agree that the apostle Paul was a great example of a person who lived a sacrificial life. The above verse is probably his life text. Let us look at the three bold phrases in this verse to glean some insight on the subject of willful sacrificial living.

"Spend" – In the Greek it is a future tense verb that may also be translated "will spend." Here Paul is saying that he will expend or consume his energy for the Corinthian church.

"Be Spent" – This is also a future tense verb which may be translated "will be utterly spent." Paul was willing to give of his utmost for the sake of the Gospel and these Corinthian Christians. Here Paul literally states that he is willing to give his all, which is a true sacrificial mindset.

"The less I be loved" – Here again Paul is stating that as the spiritual father of the church, he is willing to give his all for the church. As usual, those who give the most always seem to reap the least rewards in the area of appreciation. I would also like to offer a secondary meaning to this phrase. Paul is giving so much love to the Corinthians that he has placed himself second in terms of concern. Any person who is willing to be utterly spent for the Lord is a person who has placed their own creature comforts on the back burner.

Another hallmark verse on sacrificing is 1 Thessalonians 2:8: *"Having so fond an affection for you, we were well-pleased to impart to you not only the gospel of God but also our own lives, because you had become very dear to us."*

JESUS MODELED SERVANT LEADERSHIP

Jesus is the greatest picture of **leadership** and its impact on people and the world. His way of leading was as a servant. We see many times and aspects of Jesus serving people. We will examine five such times and draw a parallel to the practice of serving as a leader.

In Matthew 9:35-38 we read, *"Jesus was going through all the cities and villages, teaching in their synagogues and proclaiming the gospel of the kingdom, and healing every kind of disease and every kind of sickness. Seeing the people, He felt compassion for them, because they were distressed and dispirited like sheep without a shepherd. Then He said to His disciples, "The harvest is plentiful, but the workers are few. Therefore beseech the Lord of the harvest to send out workers into His harvest."*

We see Jesus having a compassion on the people because He saw their needs. He knew He was sent to meet those needs and also that He would train and send others to meet the needs of the people, whom he likened to a harvest. This example shows His servant heart and also how He focused action to meet the needs. His heart was captured in Mark 10:45, *"For even the Son of Man did not come to be served, but to serve, and to give His life a ransom for many."*

Jesus served people by **inspiring** them and giving them a **vision** for the future. We especially see this when Jesus is preparing to leave and the disciples are confused. He gives them a hope about the future and their role in it. *"And Jesus came up and spoke to them, saying, 'All authority has been given to Me in heaven and on earth. Go therefore and make disciples of all the nations, baptizing them in the name of the Father and the Son and the Holy Spirit, teaching them to observe all that I commanded you; and lo, I am with you always, even to the end of the age'"* (Matthew 28:18-20).

Jesus' **posture** was one of serving and lifting others up. He paid attention to the **process** and details even as his death on the cross approached. The classic picture of this is found in John 13 at the last supper. Jesus *"got up from supper, and laid aside His garments; and taking a towel, He girded Himself. Then He poured water into the basin, and began to wash the disciples' feet and to wipe them with the towel with which He was girded....*

"So when He had washed their feet, and taken His garments and reclined at the table again, He said to them, 'Do you know what I have done to you? You call Me Teacher and Lord; and you are right, for so I am. If I then, the Lord and the Teacher, washed your feet, you also ought to wash one another's feet. For I gave you an example that you also should do as I did to you. Truly, truly, I say to you, a slave is not greater than his master, nor is one who is sent greater than the one who sent him. If you know these things, you are blessed if you do them'" (John 13:4-5, 12-17).

Next we see Jesus' incredible **heart** for people and how much He **valued people** in John 15:12-15, *"This is My commandment, that you love one another, just as I have loved you. Greater love has no one than this, that one lay down his life for his friends. You are My friends if you do what I command you. No longer do I call you slaves, for the slave does not know* *what his master is doing; but I have called you friends, for all things that I have heard from My Father I have made known to you."*

Finally we recognize Jesus had a clear sense of His mission: *"For the Son of Man has come to seek and to save that which was lost" (Luke 19:10).* Also, He was **equipping His disciples to follow** in His steps with His power: *"But you will receive power when the Holy Spirit has come upon you; and you shall be My witnesses both in Jerusalem, and in all Judea and Samaria, and even to the remotest part of the earth"* (Acts 1:8).

Jesus served all whom He came in contact with, whether it was the adulterous women at the well, the blind beggar, the cheating tax-gatherers, or the disciples themselves. In particular He served those who were in need—physical, spiritual, or relational. His goal was to introduce them into a relationship with a living God who could restore them to life. By serving them, they grew and were made whole and then were able to engage in the Father's purposes.

Jesus Christ served "The Least, The Last, and The Lost." He said in Matthew 25:40, *"The King will answer and say to them, 'Truly I say to you, to the extent that you did it to one of these brothers of Mine, even the least of them, you did it to Me.'"* All people were of equal importance and value. This meant the people He dealt with had difficulties and at times their lives were messy. He did not try to control who came in to His sphere of influence; He chose to respond and love all people.

Jesus served seekers and leaders alike. Serving is to be a heartbeat and a lifestyle. It is not to think you are better than others but instead to have eyes to see the needs of others and help however you can. It does not mean I need to meet every need I see—one cannot meet all of the needs that exist. The key is to listen to the Lord and follow where He directs and meet what needs He shows to you.

We all should have a "serving" mindset in our relationships, in our daily work, and in our roles—especially as leaders. Serving helps us focus on others as people of value rather than on simply meeting their needs.

WHY SERVANT LEADERSHIP

Serving is the most effective way to fill God's purposes because God goes to work in His power and in His way. This is far better than relying on our own strength. Serving honors the Lord and puts Him ahead of our agenda and motives. This kind of leadership reflects godly values—it is how God the Father, Jesus Christ, and Paul led. This way is proven and has changed the world. Through serving, people are brought into a greater unity and cohesiveness.

Serving is countercultural; it is not natural and will take the Spirit of God to work through you to accomplish anything. Because it is counterintuitive, it draws people's attention. It stands out in a crowded field of leadership principles.

Serving is the best way to connect people and mission. It engages people based on the fact that they are the greatest asset for any company or endeavor. Serving both harnesses the collective IQ of the team and leverages the strengths and gifts to increase the output. Because we need one another, serving connects us to one another. Serving is also the best way to connect to the next generation because they feel valued. Finally it is a scalable and sustainable model for growth.

> *"Leaders we admire do not place themselves at the center; they place others there. They do not seek the attention of people; they give it to others. They do not focus on satisfying their own aims and desires; they look for ways to respond to the needs and interests of others Being a servant may not be what many leaders had in mind when they choose to take the responsibility of their organization, but serving others is the most glorious and rewarding of all leadership tasks."*
> — James Kouzes and Barry Posner in
> *Credibility: How Leaders Gain and Lose It, Why People Demand It*

COMMUNITY

> *"Nothing is sweet or easy about community. Community is a fellowship of people who do not hide their joys and sorrows but make them visible to each other in a gesture of hope. In community we say: Life is full of gains and losses, joys and sorrows, ups and downs—but we do not have to live it alone. We want to drink our cup together and thus celebrate the truth that the wounds of our individual lives, which seem intolerable when live alone, become sources of healing when we live them as part of a fellowship of mutual care."*
>
> – Henri Nouwen

> *"The man who lives in a small community lives in a much larger world... The reason is obvious. In a large community we can choose our companions. In a small community our companions are chosen for us. Community is the place where the person you least want to live with always lives. Often we surround ourselves with the people we most want to live with, thus forming a club or clique, not a community. Anyone can form a club, it takes grace, shared vision and hard work to form a community."*
>
> – G. K. Chesterton

Others First

As we consider the "others first" principle, we need to see it involves both the individual and community. We need the input, growth, and challenge of one-on-one relationships to learn and understand the steps ahead.

The Need for Community

1. We are created as relational beings.
2. God meets our needs through a relational community.
3. We are commanded to be involved in One Another.

a. be of the same mind toward one another (Romans 12:16)

b. love one another (John 13:34-35)

c. serve one another (Galatians 5:13)

4. There is a good return for our labor. *"Two are better than one for they have a good return for your labor, a cord of three strands is not easily broken"* (Ecclesiastes 4:12 NIV).

5. We reflect God's grace. Begin to appreciate the manifold Grace of God (1 Peter 4:10).

6. The world discourages us from having relationships.

Hallmarks of Community

> *"It's easier to love humanity as a whole than to love one's neighbors."*
>
> **– Eric Hoffer, writer**

1. Authentic relationships – care for your soul (Psalm 142:1-4; reality)

2. Value and sacrifice for people – valuing people, weak or strong

3. Growing trust and safety

4. Building up of one another – investing in each other (Ephesians 4)

5. Healing emotionally – forgive and comfort (2 Corinthians 1:3-4; Matthew 5)

6. Weakness is the glue not just the strengths (2 Corinthians 12:9-12)

7. Accept differences – able to work through conflict and differences

8. Value diversity – the parts of the Body (1 Corinthians 12)

9. Love is a witness to the world (John 12:32)

Community is the Bridge from Intimacy to Ministry

Examine Luke 6:12-19. *"It was at this time that He went off to the mountain to pray, and He spent the whole night in prayer to God. And when day came, He called His disciples to Him and chose twelve of them, whom*

He also named as apostles: Simon, whom He also named Peter, and Andrew his brother; and James and John; and Philip and Bartholomew; and Matthew and Thomas; James the son of Alphaeus, and Simon who was called the Zealot; Judas the son of James, and Judas Iscariot, who became a traitor.

"Jesus came down with them and stood on a level place; and there was a large crowd of His disciples, and a great throng of people from all Judea and Jerusalem and the coastal region of Tyre and Sidon, who had come to hear Him and to be healed of their diseases; and those who were troubled with unclean spirits were being cured. And all the people were trying to touch Him, for power was coming from Him and healing them all."

Night to Morning to Afternoon		
Night	Alone with God, prayer, intimacy with God	INTIMACY
Morning	Gathered the men, a team, people focus	COMMUNITY
Afternoon	Went out to the world, heal disease, word	MINISTRY

Aloneness is the greatest obstacle to Community.

"Americans are the loneliest people in the world."
— Mother Theresa

Personal Keys to Overcoming Aloneness

1. Act in obedience.
2. Recognize your need.
3. Reach out and partner with others – include them in the work.
4. Find a "safe place."
5. Be accountable to those whom you trust.

Ministering to Aloneness

In ministering to aloneness we see that Christ is with us to help others. *"And He who sent Me is with Me; He has not left Me **alone**, for I always do the things that are pleasing to Him John 12:24 Truly, truly, I say to you, unless a grain of wheat falls into the earth and dies, it remains **alone**; but if it dies, it bears much fruit"* (John 8:29).

Ministering to another's aloneness requires us to do three things:

Cry – Romans 12:15

Care – Romans. 12: 9-10; 1 Corinthians 12:25

Comfort – 2 Corinthians 1:3-4

> *"Care is the participation in the pain, sharing the suffering and brokenness. Cure without care is as dehumanizing as a gift given with a cold heart. Care means to be present to each other. They listen to you, they speak to you, they ask questions of you. Their presence is a healing presence because they accept you on your terms. Our tendency is to run away from the painful realities or to try to change them as soon as possible. But cure without care makes us into rulers, controllers, manipulators, and prevents a real community from taking shape. Cure without care makes us preoccupied with quick changes, impatient and unwilling to share each other's burden."*
>
> – Henri Nouwen

> *"Beneath all our problems there are desperately hurting souls that must find the nourishment only community can provide or die. The greatest need in modern civilization is the development of communities—true communities where the heart of God is home, where the humble and wise learn to shepherd those on the path behind them, where trusting strugglers lock arms with others as together they journey on."*
>
> – Larry Crabb

Ministry will Always Involve Sacrifice

For the follower of Christ, ministry is never optional—it is a calling for all believers, not merely a subset of "professionals." Laypeople bypass abundant ministry opportunities when they stumble over the assumption that if they cannot teach or preach, they are limited to vicarious ministry through their financial support of those who can. This spectator mentality causes people to overlook the God-given circumstances and abilities with which they have been entrusted. All believers can be involved in some aspect of discipleship, even if this is limited to their families. No arena is insignificant, since reward is based on faithfulness to opportunity rather than the size of our ministry. We stunt our growth when we fail to serve others with eternal values at heart.

Remember and embrace the words of the Lord Jesus: *"Calling them to Himself, Jesus said to them, 'You know that those who are recognized as rulers of the Gentiles lord it over them; and their great men exercise authority over them. But it is not this way among you, but whoever wishes to become great among you shall be your servant; and whoever wishes to be first among you shall be slave of all. For even the Son of Man did not come to be served, but to serve, and to give His life a ransom for many'"* (Mark 10:42-45).

Jesus' last and Great Commission: *"Go therefore and make disciples of all the nations, baptizing them in the name of the Father and the Son and the Holy Spirit, teaching them to observe all that I commanded you; and lo, I am with you always, even to the end of the age"* (Matthew 28:19-20).

The Ministry is about People

We are called to serve the least, the last, and the lost. The practical expression of being generous will be focused on serving and helping people. We give way to God's plan which is always about people. This is the picture of Christ dying for each of us. He died not just to take away sins but to provide a way for people to be back in relationship to God Himself.

We must be disciples to make disciples.

> "The more we know Christ, the better we can make Him known. When Paul told the Corinthians 'I determined to know nothing among you except Jesus Christ, and Him crucified' (1 Corinthians 2:2), he saw himself as a messenger who was sent to introduce the people of Corinth to a Person with whom he had an intimate relationship. He wanted them to be more impressed with Jesus than they were with him, but this required a personal introduction to Jesus, not a list of His attributes. We must know Christ as a Person before we can guide others to this level of spiritual intimacy."
>
> — Ken Boa

We are all called to be a light in our arenas of influence. It is not optional. In fact, we are always a witness, whether we like it or not, because people will be watching. Thus we need to be intentional and be prepared to give an answer.

APPLICATION
A Lifestyle Ministry of Evangelism and Discipleship

Evangelism is most effective in a relational lifestyle. *"You are the salt of the earth; but if the salt has become tasteless, how can it be made salty again? It is no longer good for anything, except to be thrown out and trampled under foot by men. You are the light of the world. A city set on a hill cannot be hidden, nor does anyone light a lamp, and put it under a basket, but on the lampstand, and it gives light to all who are in the house. Let your light shine before men in such a way that they may see your good works, and glorify your Father who is in heaven"* (Matthew 5:12-16).

What is the purpose of salt? Of light? Why does Jesus teach about salt and light directly after the beatitudes?

The good works includes caring, listening and learning not fixing, telling or pushing an agenda.

Living among the Lost – Establish Common Ground

"*In Him was life, and the life was the Light of men*" (John 1:4). The believers in the group have Christ living in them. He is the life and this life is a light to others. Unbelievers live in a state of total spiritual blindness and imprisonment—it is our responsibility to bring the light of Christ into their darkness. A right view of their condition will help us gain a heart of compassion and wisdom that will equip us to navigate the darkness and reach them. We must remember where we came from to be effective (see Ephesians 2:1-3; 5:8).

Promises Associated with Sacrifice

In this passage from Isaiah 58:10-12 we see a number of promises for those who sacrifice and give their lives to others.

> "*And if you give yourself to the hungry*
> *And satisfy the desire of the afflicted,*
> *Then your light will rise in darkness*
> *And your gloom will become like midday.*
>
> "*And the Lord will continually guide you,*
> *And satisfy your desire in scorched places,*
> *And give strength to your bones;*
> *And you will be like a watered garden,*
> *And like a spring of water whose waters do not fail.*
>
> "*Those from among you will rebuild the ancient ruins;*
> *You will raise up the age-old foundations;*
> *And you will be called the repairer of the breach,*
> *The restorer of the streets in which to dwell.*"

SUMMARY

Sacrifice puts others ahead of self through serving. Serve others, and learn and receive from others. Leverage your life impact, make disciples, and leave a legacy.

- **Step 1 – Be missional and ministry minded.** Have clarity about "why you go to work." Rest and play to restore.
- **Step 2 – Pursue and create community.** Resolve conflicts. We need one another. Value people above all else.
- **Step 3 – Serve, invest, and empower in all of your relationships.** Give your life away. Share Christ and make disciples.
- **Step 4 – Believe the best about others and want the best for them.** Be selfless. Allow yourself to be vulnerable.

True leadership is found in serving. (See Matthew 20:26-28.)
Give and it will be given to you. (See Luke 6:38.)

Chapter 13

THE MOUNTAIN OF ETERNITY

"Receive the Realty of Life Today and Live It Forever"

KEY DESCRIPTOR: The Kingdom

CHARACTERISTICS: Legacy and Reward

ETERNITY IS A REALITY OF LIFE THAT IS RECEIVED TODAY AND FOREVER – MATTHEW 13:18-51

The Mountain of **ETERNITY** and God's Kingdom need to be where we focus our attention and effort. It is not about building kingdoms on earth and constructing a large organization or company. These are means to an end whereas God's kingdom and purposes should be our end and shape our goals.

God has never been pleased with the proud, boastful and overconfident. We know that Lucifer in his madness became Satan. He wanted to be exalted like God but he fell! The Most High God sees to it that all who will desire to be exalted contrary to His will and timing will ultimately fall. What a contrast Satan and his children present to Christ, who humbled Himself but was exalted! (See Philippians 2:8-9.)

The quality of our eternity is based on our faithfulness in life in the temporal. Letting go of the temporal, empties the hand to receive the eternal.

- Humble yourself to be honored (James 4:10).
- True leadership is found in serving (Matthew 20:26-28).

"What we do in this life, echoes in eternity!"
– Maximus

"You have not lived today until you have done something for someone who can never repay you."
– John Bunyan

HEAVEN IS OUR HOME

C. S. Lewis wrote in the *The Problem of Pain*, "Our Father refreshes us on the journey with some pleasant inns, but will not encourage us to mistake them for home." We are made for another world because we are spiritual beings at our core. We are made in the image of God and God transcends this world. We live here as guests or visitors. Heaven is our home and destination, so don't become so comfortable in this life or allow your roots to be so deep that leaving will be a tragedy.

Benefits of an Eternal Life over a Temporal Life

When we possess our new nature and our spirit is indwelt by the Holy Spirit, we gain many benefits and advantages that are simply not possible for a nonbeliever. The following are ten such attributes that we gain:

1. **Security** – our security is in the unchanging Christ and not in the accolades of the world
2. **Significance** – our worth is based on the price God paid for us (Christ) not on our possessions or position
3. **Satisfaction** – our fulfillment is found in eternal things not the temporal
4. **Power** – our power comes from the infinite power of Christ rather than our limited resources
5. **Life** – we gain a life that lives on into eternity with God rather than holding on to a physical life on earth
6. **Wisdom** – God says He will give us His wisdom, which is far greater than our own

7. **Vision** – vision comes from God who is beyond time and space versus our limited perspective

8. **Love** – we are loved unconditionally and forever by God rather than the conditional love of people

9. **Wholeness** – an eternal life makes us whole and we are restored to function

10. **Peace** – God becomes our peace because we give up control and rest in Him

> *"People think they want pleasure, recognition, popularity, status, and power, but the pursuit of these things leads, in the final analysis, to emptiness, delusion, and foolishness. God has set eternity in our hearts (Ecclesiastes 3:11), and our deepest desires are fulfillment (love, joy, peace), reality (that which does not fade away), and wisdom (skill in living). The only path to this true fulfillment lies in the conscious choice of God's value system over that which is offered by this world. This choice is based on trusting a Person we have not yet seen. 'And though you have not seen Him, you love Him, and though you do not see Him now, but believe in Him, you greatly rejoice with joy inexpressible and full of glory, obtaining as the outcome of your faith the salvation of your souls' (1 Peter 1:8-9)."*
>
> — Ken Boa, *Conformed to His Image*

ABANDON YOUR LIFE

We must continually "Die to Self" (Luke 9:23) and seek the Kingdom of God (Matthew 6:33). This is an every day battle, and we will need the life of Christ in us to be victorious.

We Live in a World of Two Opposing Economies – God's Economy vs. Man's Economy. The Bible teaches that we live and work in two worlds and two different economies at the same time.

Jesus said to Pilate: *"My kingdom is not of this world..."* (John 18:36).

> *"Come, all you who are thirsty, come to the waters; and you who have no money, come, buy and eat! Come, buy wine and milk without money and without cost"* (Isaiah 55:1-2 NIV).
>
> *"'For my thoughts are not your thoughts, neither are your ways my ways,' declares the LORD. 'As the heavens are higher than the earth, so are my ways higher than your ways and my thoughts than your thoughts'"* (Isaiah 55:8-9 NIV).
>
> *"No one can serve two masters. Either you will hate the one and love the other, or you will be devoted to the one and despise the other. You cannot serve both God and money"* (Matthew 6:24 NIV).

God's economy has nothing to do with money! Money has nothing to do with the reality of true satisfaction. "Mammon" or the power of money competes for our allegiance and tries to destroy relationships. We sometimes ask, "Why did Jesus allow Himself to be sold for money?" He allowed Himself (once and for all) to be subject to man's economy, allowing Himself to be sold and bought, so He could break right through the powers of man's economy and set us free—allowing us to come into God's economy!

Our world is marked by the pursuit of money. *"But mark this: There will be terrible times in the last days. People will be lovers of themselves, lovers of money, boastful, proud, abusive, disobedient to their parents, ungrateful, unholy, without love, unforgiving, slanderous, without self-control, brutal, not lovers of the good, treacherous, rash, conceited, lovers of pleasure rather than lovers of God—having a form of godliness but denying its power. Have nothing to do with such people"* (2 Timothy 3:1-4 NIV).

> *"The Pharisees, who loved money, heard all this and were sneering at Jesus. He said to them, "You are the ones who justify yourselves in the eyes of others, but God knows your hearts. What people value highly is detestable in God's sight"* (Luke 16:14-15 NIV).

We need to understand God's economy is giving/receiving and the world economy is buying/selling.

Overflow always meant to bless others not to spend it on ourselves. That is the reason why God wanted to make Israel great and wealthy—to be a blessing to the nations so that they would be jealous and want to know the One True God.

Money will not protect us from problems. *"As goods increase, so do those who consume them. And what benefit are they to the owners except to feast their eyes on them?"* (Ecclesiastes 5:10 NIV). Money will never solve financial problems. It may alleviate the symptoms for a short while, but financial problems are a matter of the heart.

An Eternal Perspective – Keep the Big Picture in Focus

Our lives are but a dot on an infinite time line. We need to see that our life on earth is but a moment so we live for the eternal while in the temporal world. We then will value all of the things in this life from God's viewpoint and not man's measuring stick. We can conclude the following: eternity gives meaning to time, our destiny defines the journey we are on, and adversity drives us to dependency.

REWARDS IN HEAVEN – WE WILL REAP A REWARD IN ETERNITY

Our life on earth will affect our life in eternity. If we invest in the lives of people and do so with a right motive, we will reap rewards in heaven. It is a motivator to focus on the eternal rather than the temporal. Rewards in heaven are unlimited, thus we don't compete or compare with others on the amount of rewards they receive or we receive. God will determine how they are dispensed based on our heart and motive.

Crowns

Note the crowns that are available to the believer who lives with a Kingdom perspective.

"For who is our hope or joy or crown of exultation? Is it not even you, in the presence of our Lord Jesus at His coming? For you are our glory and joy" (1 Thessalonians 2:19-20).

"And when the Chief Shepherd appears, you will receive the unfading crown of glory" (1 Peter 5:4).

"Everyone who competes in the games exercises self-control in all things. They then do it to receive a perishable wreath, but we an imperishable" (1 Corinthians 9:25).

"Blessed is a man who perseveres under trial; for once he has been approved, he will receive the crown of life which the Lord has promised to those who love Him" (James 1:12).

"In the future there is laid up for me the crown of righteousness, which the Lord, the righteous Judge, will award to me on that day; and not only to me, but also to all who have loved His appearing" (2 Timothy 4:8).

AN ETERNAL PERSPECTIVE IN THE MIDST OF DIFFICULTIES

We briefly looked at 2 Timothy 3:1, *"But realize this, that in last days difficult times will come."* This is from Paul's very last letter that he wrote. He knew his departure was near and his time on earth was at an end. So chapters three and four, the last two chapters of Paul's letter, hold great significance for how we are to finish well and what is most important.

This verse says "the last days" or it could mean "the latter days." As we look around our world today it is easy to see and conclude that the days in which we live are the latter days if not the last days. So what was Paul's message to Timothy—how was he to handle himself and what should his perspective be?

Paul begins by telling Timothy to "realize" the days in which he would find himself. To realize means to understand the times like the men of

Issachar (1 Chronicles 12:32), see life for the reality of what is going on. We discovered this in chapter one—there is a gathering storm. In addition, Paul notes in Ephesians 5:15, "that the days are evil"—there is a spiritual battle going on. We will face difficulty, persecution, and pain. Don't despair—keep looking up.

Paul's message to Timothy was "wake up and be on guard," for the enemy crouches at the door to "kill, steal, and destroy." We need to wake up from our consuming busyness and endless distraction of entertainment to be wise and pursue the eternal. We do this by finding "hope" in the storm and by finding the hope of Christ. From the hope of Christ we then exercise faith and love.

Immediately, Paul begins to describe in 2 Timothy 3:2-9 those we should not hang out with. He details 20 characteristics of such people, including those *"holding to a form of godliness, although they have denied its power. Avoid such men as these...always learning and never able to come to the knowledge of the truth...so these men also oppose the truth, men of depraved mind."* Bad company will tear you down and influence you to make bad decisions.

The community we surround ourselves with is critical in challenging times. Hebrews talks about *"not forsaking our own assembling together, as is the habit of some, but encouraging one another; and all the more as you see the day drawing near"* (Hebrews 10:25). We will need their encouragement, strength, and wisdom in the battle. The enemy wants us to be alone so he can take us out. There is strength in numbers. We need the "hope of one another" (see 1 Thessalonians 2:19-20). We **need** community and relationships.

Paul then instructs Timothy that he will need a committed, personal relationship with Christ (see 2 Timothy 3:10-17). We are to do three things. First, **Follow Him and His teaching**—*"Now you followed my teaching, conduct, purpose, faith, patience, love, perseverance, persecutions, and sufferings."* Second, **Press on,** knowing that *"all who desire to live godly in Christ Jesus will be persecuted."* Thirdly, **Continue in the Word**—*"Continue in the things you have learned and become convinced of...Scripture equips us*

145

for every good work."

In the latter days we will need to seek an intense walk of faith. We must seek to walk in a manner worthy of the Lord. God's Word will guide our attitude and perspective. It says in Romans 15:4 that God's Word is our hope.

Then, in 2 Timothy 4:1-5 Paul instructs Timothy to **carry on and practice ministry**—*"preach the word; be ready in season and out of season...be sober in all things, endure hardship, do the work of an evangelist, fulfill your ministry."* We all have a gifting and calling which is found in our purpose. Write it out and fulfill it. Teach the truth and don't tickle the ears. We are all called to serve in an intentional ministry in the problems. It takes our focus off of ourselves and it actually helps others. Be engaged in sharing Christ in the trials because that is when people are open. The bottom line is to know our purpose and calling. (See Ephesians 2:10 and Matthew 5:16.)

The fourth principle Paul gives to Timothy is **persevere and complete your mission – have a kingdom perspective**—*"Fight the good fight, Finish the course, keep the faith...In the future there is laid up for me the crown of righteousness...to all who have loved His appearing"* (2 Timothy 4:6-8; 16-18). The Lord will stand with you when all else will fall away. Glorify the Lord in your life, and press on in spite of the difficulties.

When we keep looking for the second coming of Christ, there will be a hope and vision that comes with it. Let this guide your perspective and thus your activity. Keep focused on the Kingdom, not on the externals. Night is closing in; don't go to sleep. Be prepared and on the alert.

Paul then shares a final personal note of God's amazing love and strength. He calls us to **overcome**—*"The Lord stood with me and strengthened me, so that through me the proclamation might be fully accomplished, and that all the Gentiles might hear; and I was rescued out of the lion's mouth. The Lord will rescue me from every evil deed, and will bring me safely to His heavenly kingdom..."* (2 Timothy 4:17-18). We are not alone—Christ lives in and through us. He will stand with us, strengthen us, accomplish His work, rescue us, and bring us safely to the Kingdom.

MISSION – SHARE THE GOSPEL
BECAUSE PEOPLE NEED THE LORD

We are called to be active in living among the "lost." The Lord has placed each of us in a special and unique setting—a family, a community, and workplace. Think on how the Lord can use you as a light in that context.

"Let your light shine before men in such a way they may see your good works and glorify your father who is in heaven" (Matthew 5:16). The good works includes caring, listening and learning not fixing, telling or pushing an agenda.

"In Him was life, and the life was the Light of men" (John 1:4). The believers in the group have Christ living in them. He is the life and this life is a light to others.

"The King will answer and say to them, 'Truly I say to you, to the extent that you did it to one of these brothers of Mine, even the least of them, you did it to Me'" (Matthew 25:40).

Christ had a passion and a compassion to reach the lost. Paul indicated in 1 Corinthians 9:19-23 that he became all things to all men the he might save some. His heart and conviction was not just to preach the gospel or share Christ with the "lost," but also to live among the lost—to be there for them. He wanted to develop meaningful relationships with them in such a way that questions would arise.

Pray for opportunities to share your story of faith. Our faith journey in the area of finances can be one of the best ways to start a conversation with a seeker. Ask the Lord to open doors and for people to see a difference in your life and what is your hope. *"But sanctify Christ as Lord in your hearts, always being ready to make a defense to everyone who asks you to give an account for the hope that is in you, yet with gentleness and reverence"* (1 Peter 3:15).

SUMMARY

Eternity is a reality that is received today and lived forever. Lay up treasures and gain perspective. (Perspective: let go of the temporal, have a Kingdom focus, leave people who will carry on.)

Step 1 – Develop an eternal/Kingdom mindset. Let this frame your value system. Seek eternal treasure and reward.

Step 2 – Have clarity and be living your purpose and calling. Know who and whose you are.

Step 3 – Realize we all will leave everything behind. Make sure your life is more about people than possessions or play.

Step 4 – Be "all in" on eternity—now and forever. Seek first the Kingdom. Heaven is our true home.

Humble yourself to be honored. (See James 4:10.)
God's Kingdom is not of this world. (See John 15:19, 18:36; Romans 12:2.)

Chapter 14

THE VALLEY OF TAKE ACTION

"Persevere, motivated by hope to finish well."
KEY DESCRIPTOR: Faithfulness
CHARACTERISTICS: Pressing In and Pressing On

Lose your life for God's sake and you will find it (see Matthew 10:39). We are aliens in exile (see Philippians 3:20).

As we focus on God's Kingdom and the eternal things in our temporal world, we need to press on and persevere to be able to finish well. This takes place in the Valley of **TAKE ACTION**. We should all desire to hear "Well done, good and faithful servant." Finishing well honors the Lord and ushers us into heaven itself.

People try to find the meaning of life in earthly pursuits—trying to succeed and prosper, and trying to enjoy their material possessions—only to find out too late that nothing on earth really satisfies the soul. Friend, without Jesus, life is meaningless, because Jesus is the very essence of life. He is everything that your poor lost soul has ever longed for. Jesus will still be Lord and King even without you, but friend you are nothing without Jesus!

Finishing well requires faithfully pressing in and pressing on in hope in spite of the pain and circumstances.

PRESS IN

To "press in" is to lean in and lean towards the Lord. Even if it is painful and uncomfortable, we need to rely upon the Lord.

> "When you first begin to exercise, it's somewhat painful. Not wildly painful, like touching a hot stove, but enough that if your only goal was to avoid pain, you certainly would stop doing it. But if you keep exercising...well, it just keeps getting more painful. When you're done, if you've really pushed yourself, you often feel exhausted and sore. And the next morning it's even worse.
>
> "If that was all that happened, you'd probably never do it. It's not that much fun being sore. Yet we do it anyway—because we know that, in the long run, the pain will make us stronger. Next time we'll be able to run harder and lift more before the pain starts.
>
> "And knowing this makes all the difference. Indeed, we come to see the pain as a sort of pleasure—it feels good to really push yourself, to fight through the pain and make yourself stronger. Feel the burn! It's fun to wake up sore the next morning, because you know that's just a sign that you're getting stronger."
>
> – Aaron Swartz

Pressing in to the Lord is to be at home with Him and continually exercising the spiritual disciplines of prayer, Bible study, listening, etc. Pressing in to Him takes us away from the continual draw and clamor of the world. We are in the world but not of the world (John 17:14-16).

PRESS ON

"Not that I have already obtained it or have already become perfect, but I press on so that I may lay hold of that for which also I was laid hold of by Christ Jesus. Brethren, I do not regard myself as having laid hold of it yet; but one thing I do: forgetting what lies behind and reaching forward to what lies ahead, I press on toward the goal for the prize of the upward call of God in Christ Jesus" (Philippians 3:12-14).

- Lose you life for God's sake and you will find it (Matthew 10:39).
- The last will be made first (Matthew 19:30).

KEEP YOUR EYES ON YOUR TRUE HOME

Our home is heaven and a relationship with Christ in and for eternity. Consider life and ending for Paul, Stephen, Jesus, and the faithful saints listed in Hebrews 11. Remember, we can't change our past, but we can transform our lives and our stories by placing them into God's grand story. *"'For I know the plans that I have for you,' declares the Lord, 'plans for welfare and not for calamity to give you a future and a hope'"* (Jeremiah 29:11).

DETERMINE TO FINISH WELL

Finally, are you committed to finishing your life well? Put your hand to endeavors that extend God's Kingdom. The following are ten keys to finishing well. It is not easy, yet can be obtained if one is faithful.

1. A white-hot passion and a growing, intimate relationship with the Lord – Christ as life, exercising the spiritual disciplines, ministry to God, worship, and praise.
2. A humble spirit – know your strengths and weaknesses. Always be thankful in everything.
3. Healthy relationships with spouse and family – resolve conflict, work through emotions, provide loving care.
4. Be a part of a community with humble, broken believers.
5. A simple lifestyle – be debt free, beware of entanglement in money or possessions, practice contentment, and practice enjoyment.

6. A way of life that demonstrates God's ownership and our stewardship that grows into a radical generosity focused on living God's purposes of helping others. Life is not about you.

7. A clear sense of purpose and calling that leads you to priorities, margin, and wise decisions.

8. Being others centered by engaging in a ministry of discipleship and evangelism.

9. Continue to be a learner – read, learn new things, engage your mind and heart.

10. Keep focused on God's kingdom – God at work, spiritual battles, and the Second Coming; Eternal vs. temporal; Biblical perspective of life.

Commitment:

Pray for the lost around you. Ask the Lord to open a door to share your hope.

SUMMARY

Take action and persevere to finish will, motivated by hope. Press on; don't quit (follow, faithfulness, finishing well, and having tenacity).

Step 1 – Be faithful to the opportunities God provides. Live in the moment. Be all there.

Step 2 – Live well and finish well. It takes focus, sacrifice, and going against the majority.

Step 3 – Persevere in spite of all the ups and downs. Press on and press in to the Lord. He will sustain you.

Step 4 – Be prepared for spiritual warfare. Put on the armor; resist the enemy; be on guard.

Lose your life for God's sake and you will find it. (See Matthew 10:39.)
We are aliens in exile, citizens of heaven. (See Philippians 3:20.)

Chapter 15

MAKING A DIFFERENCE

ENGAGING IN THE WARFARE

As followers of Christ, we are involved in an all-encompassing conflict, whether we know it or not. Conflicts with the worldly and demonic systems are external to believers, but they entice and provide opportunities for the flesh, which is the capacity for sin within us.

Christ has already won the victory, but until He returns, the battle still rages on three fronts: the world, the flesh, and the devil (see Ephesians 2:2-3).

1. **The world**. *"In the world you have tribulation, but take courage; I have overcome the world"* (John 16:33b). *"For whatever is born of God overcomes the world; and this is the victory that has overcome the world—our faith"* (1 John 5:4).

2. **The flesh**. *"But I say, walk by the Spirit, and you will not carry out the desire of the flesh. For the flesh sets its desire against the Spirit, and the Spirit against the flesh; for these are in opposition to one another, so that you may not do the things that you please"* (Galatians 5:16-17).

3. **The devil**. *"...The ruler of this world has been judged"* (John 16:11b). *"...The word of God abides in you, and you have overcome the evil one...greater is He who is in you than he who is in the world"* (1 John 2:14b; 4:4b).

Note the description of the battle in the book of Ephesians, *"Finally, be strong in the Lord and in the strength of His might. Put on the full armor of God, that you will be able to stand firm against the schemes of the devil. For our struggle is not against flesh and blood, but against the rulers, against the powers, against the world forces of this darkness, against the spiritual forces of wickedness in the heavenly places. Therefore, take up the full armor of God, so that you will be able to resist in the evil day, and having done everything, to stand firm"* (Ephesians 6:10-13).

The New Testament exhorts us to realize that a war is going on, to recognize the strategies of the enemy, and to know how to fight. It is important that we maintain a biblical balance as we consider the warfare. "There are two equal and opposite errors into which our race can fall about the devils. One is to disbelieve in their existence. The other is to believe, and to feel an excessive and unhealthy interest in them. They themselves are equally pleased by both errors" (C. S. Lewis, Preface to *The Screwtape Letters*). Those who ignore the biblical teaching about the reality of the enemy and the weapons of the warfare put themselves in a dangerous position of vulnerability.

"For though we walk in the flesh, we do not war according to the flesh, for the weapons of our warfare are not of the flesh, but divinely powerful for the destruction for fortresses" (2 Corinthians 10:3-4). This spiritual warfare is an every day process; sometimes we are aware of it and sometimes not. As we seek and follow the Lord, the target on our back grows. We are not only participating in the battle, we become the focus of the enemy's wrath. We never have enough strength or wisdom to combat the enemy in ourselves, and that's why we need an intimate walk with the Lord in order to unleash His power to fight through us.

> *"Paul exhorts us to 'put on the full armor of God' so that we can 'stand firm against the schemes of the devil' (Ephesians 6:11). This metaphor makes it clear that the spiritual warfare is proactive; we must be prepared, ready to resist, and empowered to advance into enemy territory. Christ is the Victor who calls us to stand on the ground He has won through His blood.*

As long as we are prepared for battle, we need not retreat before any intruder. It is wise to pray on the armor of God each morning, because without it we are open to attack."

— Ken Boa

DEPENDENT ON GOD'S PRESENCE

Those who wait on the Lord...shall walk and not faint.
ISAIAH 40:31

There is no thrill for us in walking, yet it is the test for all of our steady and enduring qualities. To "walk and not faint" is the highest stretch possible as a measure of strength. The word *walk* is used in the Bible to express the character of a person— "...John...looking at Jesus as He walked...said, 'Behold the Lamb of God!'" (John 1:35-36). There is nothing abstract or obscure in the Bible; everything is vivid and real. God does not say, "Be spiritual," but He says, "Walk before Me..." (Genesis 17:1).

When we are in an unhealthy condition either physically or emotionally, we always look for thrills in life. In our physical life this leads to our efforts to counterfeit the work of the Holy Spirit; in our emotional life it leads to obsessions and to the destruction of our morality; and in our spiritual life, if we insist on pursuing only thrills, on mounting up "with wings like eagles" (Isaiah 40:31), it will result in the destruction of our spirituality.

Having the reality of God's presence is not dependent on our being in a particular circumstance or place, but is only dependent on our determination to keep the Lord before us continually. Our problems arise when we refuse to place our trust in the reality of His presence. The experience the psalmist speaks of— "We will not fear, even though..." (Psalm 46:2)—

> will be ours once we are grounded on the truth of the reality of God's presence, not just a simple awareness of it, but an understanding of the reality of it. Then we will exclaim, "He has been here all the time!" At critical moments in our lives it is necessary to ask God for guidance, but it should be unnecessary to be constantly saying, "Oh, Lord, direct me in this, and in that." Of course He will, and in fact, He is doing it already! If our everyday decisions are not according to His will, He will press through them, bringing restraint to our spirit. Then we must be quiet and wait for the direction of His presence.
>
> — Oswald Chambers from *My Utmost for His Highest Updated Edition*

WHERE ARE YOU?
Ask, Assess, Act, and Appropriate – Take Hold and Possess

Appropriating "Christ in us" is the critical factor at each stage of life. He has given us everything that pertains to life and godliness; He is our hope and strength. Appropriation is taking hold and living by the means that Christ has given to us (love, grace, strength, relationships). Appropriation is by faith, discipline, applying His Word and growing up in Him. The journey through the stages of mountains and valleys is a growth process.

The variable for each of us is how we live this "Christ Life." Are we faithful and obedient? Do we seek His will and Kingdom above our desires? Are we serving others? Have we given up ownership and become stewards of the time, talent, treasure, truth, relationships, and grace that has been given us? Are we exercising loving God, self, and others? What is our perspective of the trials and our true home? These are just a few of the questions and hurdles we will encounter.

We are promised that we can have and can experience an abundant life—a life filled with Christ, the fruit of the Spirit, grace, and hope. As we have said, appropriating these requires our commitment and progress.

This is not a life without challenges, hurt, pain, and difficulty. Yet it is a journey to ultimate victory!

MASTER THE MOUNTAINS AND EXPERIENCE VICTORY IN THE VALLEYS

The journey is long and arduous, full of difficulties and setbacks as well as progress and triumphs. As we climb the mountains, we are called to master them, using the skills God provides to flourish in each step along the way. In the valleys we are to have victory, which means we live in the peace and strength of God, growing in faith and learning each step of the way. The final victory is to enjoy the Lord and His reward in eternity along with a rich legacy. *"No, despite all these things, overwhelming victory is ours through Christ, who loved us"* (Romans 8:37 NLT).

Appendix

LESSONS IN MOUNTAINS AND VALLEYS

MOUNTAINS

1. Only mountaintops give us perspective of both where we have been and where we are going.
2. Everyone who goes up must come down. We ascend and descend.
3. One cannot live on mountaintops – there is little or no food, water or people (even sometimes air). The growth in surrounding life actually decreases as one ascends.
4. Footing diminishes as one climbs. There are fewer places of rest.
5. The mountaintops or highs of life are times to be celebrated yet not worshipped. We can't make a life out of mountaintop experiences.
6. Climbing mountains builds our stamina and strength.
7. When climbing the mountains, one cannot see but a few steps ahead and many steps behind.
8. When descending the mountains we see little behind and the long road ahead.
9. From a distance mountains and mountaintops look easy to climb and close. They generally never are.

VALLEYS

1. Valleys represent the journey of brokenness and surrender. Only through brokenness and surrender can life, power, and the Spirit of Christ flow. Grace is made manifest – 2 Corinthians 12:9-10.
2. Trials and pain are the path to true maturity and growth – James 1:2-4

3. Difficulties and struggles (pain) are always redemptive when seen from God's viewpoint – He is doing a work – Romans 8:28.

4. We learn dependence, abiding, the value of people and the blessing or perseverance through the valleys.

5. True ministry flows from being comforted in our affliction – 2 Corinthians 1:3-4.

6. The Lord never leaves us in our pain – He is always present.

7. In brokenness and surrender we are confronted with our weakness. Only by weakness is power manifested.

8. Weakness, pain, and trials must be embraced, or we will not learn the lesson and thus be destined to repeat it.

9. Ask "What?" and not "Why?" – "What?" points forward. "Why?" leaves us trying to be on God's level, demanding an answer from Him.

10. Victories can build walls, and failures can build bridges.

11. We tend to learn more from mistakes than we do from success.

12. Valleys drive us to dependence and growth in faith.

13. Hope is clarified in the difficult times, sustaining us in the good times.

14. In pain we identify with Christ in His sufferings and are conformed to His image.

15. Hurt and pain purify and cleanse the heart.

16. Valleys are where the food, people, water, and protection are.

17. As we progress through the mountains and valleys we bear more fruit along the way. We go from no fruit, to fruit, to more fruit, to much fruit, to multiplying fruit.

18. Trials and hurt form humility in our character. Only the humble can be secure, servant leaders. Humility is attractive, but pride repels.

19. True leadership is forged, strengthened, grown, and released in difficulties and trials. This is countercultural and counterintuitive.

20. We are already victorious in the valleys when we keep our focus on Christ – Psalm 23.

21. Brokenness and surrender are not the way of the world or even the church.
22. Wise people learn from others' mistakes and challenges.
23. Two of Satan's greatest weapons are pain and hurt, which cause division and anger, cripple us, keep us alone, and destroy others.
24. As we grow in maturity and eternity, the target on our back grows – we will encounter more spiritual opposition.
25. Our suffering is momentary and temporal when compared to eternity.
26. Persecution is said to be a blessing – we will inherit the kingdom of God.
27. We are called to take up our cross daily and die to self – this is a choice.
28. Victory only comes through surrender.
29. Our roots are deepened in drought and the desert.
30. Trials and persecution strengthen and grow the community and the body of Christ.

ABOUT THE AUTHOR

Bruce R. Witt is President of Leadership Revolution Inc., a non-profit organization dedicated to developing and multiplying servant leaders who live as Christ and mobilize others to reach their world. He began his career in marketing for Shell Oil Company in the solid plastics area. He was led to join the Christian Business Men's Committee where he directed the U.S. field operations and authored several key curriculum for the ministry, including the Operation Timothy spiritual development series and the Lighthouse evangelism curriculum.

In 2008, after seeing the tremendous need for leaders to understand and practice Christ as the Leader in their entire life, Bruce was led to form Leadership Revolution in order to establish a process that would help leaders truly allow Christ to be their leader.

Bruce has written curriculum and training resources and he regularly travels throughout the United States and the globe conducting workshops, conferences and train the trainer sessions to spread the vision and empower others to follow Christ as their leader. Along with partner organizations and churches, Bruce has trained thousands of leaders and trained hundreds of trainers who can also train others.

Bruce has been married to his wife Dana for over 30 years and they have two grown sons, Robert and Andrew.

ABOUT LEADERSHIP REVOLUTION INC.

THE PROBLEM is there's a leadership crisis, and current leadership training isn't working.

THE SOLUTION is that we begin with Christ as the One Leader. His infinite, supernatural power is released through brokenness and surrender.

OUR MISSION is to establish Christ as the One Leader in every follower. Our Vision is to transform leaders in every continent to multiply the Gospel impact.

WHO WE SERVE

We are privileged to serve these leadership groups:

33% PASTORS

33% MINISTRY LEADERS

33% BUSINESS LEADERS

We train leaders along with 16 strategic partners to follow the One Leader, Jesus Christ, and His model of leadership. We're blessed to serve and train in 17 countries including Egypt, India, Ghana, Kenya, Indonesia, Russia, China, and several Latin American countries.

Whether it's training your staff on the One Leader message or joining us a partner in ministry, please contact us to learn more.

LEADERSHIP REVOLUTION
ESTABLISHING CHRIST AS THE LEADER

LeadershipRevolution.us | 678-637-9890 | Bruce@LeadershipRevolution.us

Leadership Revolution Inc. is a 501(c)3 nonprofit. All gifts and donations are tax deductible.

THE BROADER PLAN FOR YOUR LEADERSHIP DEVELOPMENT

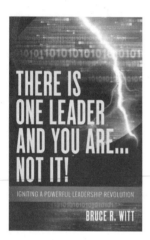

What are the greatest challenges that you face as a leader? In this in-depth, foundational book, *There is One Leader and You are....Not It!*, Bruce Witt shares the seven foundational principles that Jesus Christ, the One Leader, established to eternally impact the world around us.

ISBN 978-0-9965714-1-8
228 pages, Softcover

What Are You Giving Your Life To? provides a healthy dose of spiritual and practical guidance on understanding and following God's personal design and calling for you, how to intentionally create Kingdom-focused priorities in life and work, and the most successful ways to overcome life's challenges and obstacles.

ISBN 978-0-9965714-0-1
128 pages, Softcover